COMPANIONS IN COURAGE

COMPANIONS IN
COURAGE

Triumphant Tales of
Heroic Athletes

PAT LAFONTAINE
with Dr. Ernie Valutis, Chas Griffin,
and Larry Weisman

WARNER BOOKS

A Time Warner Company

Warner Books, Inc., 1271 Avenue of the Americas, New York, NY 10020

Visit our Web site at www.twbookmark.com

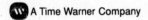 A Time Warner Company

Printed in the United States of America
First Printing: January 2001
10 9 8 7 6 5 4 3 2 1

Library of Congress Cataloging-in-Publication Data

LaFontaine, Pat.
    Companions in courage : triumphant tales of heroic athletes / Pat LaFontaine
with Ernie Valutis, Chas Griffin, and Larry Weisman.
        p. cm.
    ISBN 0-446-52705-X
    1. Athletes—United States—Biography. I. Title: Inspirational stories of athletes
who overcame the odds. II. Valutis, Erinie. III. Griffin, Chas. IV. Weisman,
Larry. V. Title.

GV697 .A1 L34 2001
796'.092'2—dc21
    [B]   00-063338

Book design by Giorgetta McRee

To the children who have fought and are fighting battles for life and health. May your bravery and courageous spirit be an inspiration to others as they have been to me.

Acknowledgments

To my companions who are no longer with us. Thank you for your courage, inspiration, and friendship.

With love and gratitude to my personal companions in life:
My best friend and wife, Marybeth.
My hat trick of inspiration, Sarah, Brianna, and Daniel.
Thank you for your love and support.

Sincere thanks to the LaFontaine and Hoey families and to the dear friends in the communities where I lived and played. A special thank you to Donnie Meehan and Marianne "Mokey" McCarthy.

To Fred, the golden retriever we had and loved for ten years. Dog lovers everywhere will understand how we miss him.

To my literary companions:
This book could not have been written without the tremendous commitment and support of a great group of people. Heartfelt thanks to my friends Chas Griffin and Dr.

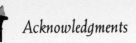

Acknowledgments

Ernie Valutis for your research, writing, and guidance. And many thanks to Rick Wolff, Larry Weisman, and Dan Ambrosio for pulling the whole project together.

To Michael J. Fox, a true gentleman in every sense of the word. Special thanks for bringing your courageous spirit to this book.

I would also like to recognize the contributions of John LaFontaine Sr., Arthur Pincus, Jim Johnson, Laurie Widzinski, John Rufer, Alan Kaufman, Warner Books, Inc., Newport Sports Management, Inc., and the National Hockey League Inc. and NHL Players' Association and their Hockey's All-Star Kids program.

Genuine appreciation to those professionals who helped keep my mind and body together during some tough times: Dr. James Kelly, Dr. Jeffrey Minkoff, Dr. Ronald Petersen, Dr. Ernie Valutis, Steve Wirth, Chris Reichart, Kevin Cichocki, and Vladimir Anoufriev.

To each of the organizations I was associated with—New York Islanders, Buffalo Sabres, New York Rangers, TEAM USA, and Verdun Juniors—and the teammates, coaches, trainers, and the many great fans.

To those athletes who have a passion for their sport as well as for helping those in need.

To all the unknown stories of courage and spirit that have yet to be told.

Pat LaFontaine
October 2000

Contents

Contents

Contents

Foreword

I've known Pat LaFontaine for a long time. Like most hockey fans (and most of you know by now that I've been an avid hockey player and fan all my life) I admired Pat for his remarkable abilities on the ice—he always knew how to put the puck in the net or how to spot a teammate and feed him a perfect pass. But as much as I admired Pat for his athletic abilities, it wasn't until we had a chance to work together on an episode of *Spin City* that I truly became impressed with Pat LaFontaine the human being.

We had asked Pat to make a cameo appearance on the show, and during the course of the shooting there was a scene in which we had to skate on the ice together. Now this was a time when Pat was recuperating from a serious head concussion and I remember thinking to myself, "Please, God, whatever I do, please don't let me accidentally knock him down!" Fortunately, my skating skills held up and Pat finished the scene with me flawlessly and, most importantly, not injured.

But it was during this time that I had a chance to get to know Pat LaFontaine well, and it was quickly apparent to me that this was a man who wanted to give a lot more to this world than just goals and assists. Pat is one of those unique people who just flat out cares about other people, and in today's world of selfish, highly egocentric "What's-in-it-for-me?" professional athletes, Pat is truly a breath of fresh air.

Up to that point, I had always followed his career. But then I really focused on Pat when he was with the New York Rangers. And when he was finally forced to retire after suffering from another collision on the ice, I sat down and wrote a heartfelt note to him.

I remember the letter quite well, because it was meant to praise Pat and to urge him to keep going in life, no matter what kinds of obstacles are thrown in his way. But in truth—and what only I knew at the time—I was really writing about my own battle with Parkinson's and, in effect, was trying to affirm my own beliefs in my competitive spirit to keep going. Pat's decision to retire and move on with his life was virtually setting the stage for my own upcoming personal battle.

That's why the people in this book and their stories mean so much to me. For the most part, these are not athletes whom you have heard of or athletes who have made fortunes from playing sports. Rather, these are rare individuals who have refused to call it quits—even when everybody else has already written them off. To me, these athletes are the *real* champions in sports, and they deserve all the encouragement we can muster.

Let me tell you a secret: I can't type. And no, it's not because of the Parkinson's. The truth is, I just can't type. Never learned how when I was a kid. So to get around this problem, I have a voice-activated computer that responds to my verbal instructions and then instantly prints my words on the computer screen. When I sat down to write this foreword, the first words that I uttered were "Companions in Courage."

When I looked at the screen, the computer printed the following:

"Companions . . . Encourage."

And I thought to myself, "What a most appropriate rewrite!"

You see, it's my experience in life that there are people who worry about getting the job done, and then there are those who just put the worries aside and get the job done. This book, *Companions in Courage*, focuses squarely on those athletes who just get it done.

In short, they represent the very best when it comes to the spirit of true athletic competition. Thank you, Pat La-Fontaine, for sharing their stories with us all.

Michael J. Fox
October 2000

Preface

We all live within a story. Our lives unfold as we experience each day, as we deal with what life serves. I am learning how to handle life's setbacks, those challenges that push us all beyond our limits and beneath the surface of life.

When my world as a professional athlete began to fall apart, I did not have the tools to deal effectively with what was happening to me. But as I started to listen to my circumstances, I began to learn from them. In the process I found a place of understanding and healing, a place where I could become a friend to myself and to others.

I discovered that there is a creative flow and rhythm that exists beneath the surface reality of life. Before my setbacks got my attention, the only freedom and flow I understood was on the surface of the ice as a professional athlete. Ironically, that other place beneath the ice was what I had always avoided—it seemed that the only way to get there was through my pain. I began to realize that I don't have to be defined by what happens to me, that I can learn to manage my circumstances instead of being controlled by them.

My Companions in Courage have taught me important lessons. I've come to understand that courage comes in many forms. I've seen small children fighting for their lives against cancer. I know teenagers and grown-ups who have survived all manner of disease and affliction and fought their wars with dignity. I know those who have felt and conquered the sting of racism and prejudice.

I want to share these lessons in the hope that this book will be your companion, that it will help you find that safe place beneath the surface of your life so that you can become your own friend and cultivate the courage it takes to manage life's twists and turns.

No, it's not easy. There's a complexity to the textures of the pattern of your life. For me, working with challenged children in hospital wards, tasting fame and fortune, feeling the helpless grief of tragedy, and knowing life's joys and sorrows make for a depth I can only hope to understand.

These experiences have taught me that we are all companions who are learning to be courageous, learning to transcend life's harsh moments in order to write our own story. I believe that what happens to each of us—what pushes us past normal existence—is what helps us find the positive, limitless purity that makes each of us who we are. Learning to bring the two sides of life together helps us open a creative personal rhythm that gives meaning and purpose to whatever life lays before us.

Each person who has crossed my path or whose story has come to my attention possesses a beauty and strength that has been a gift to me. Each is a spontaneous example of our life force in motion. This book will share my story, the stories of other athletes, and the powerful lessons we can all learn from.

These people have become my Companions in Courage, and they're the heart of this book. Some enjoy fame and popularity and wide acclaim, in stadiums and arenas and on television. Others will come to you as strangers but will become friends, mentors, guides. Their acts of personal courage occur in the toughest arena of all—everyday life.

Often, we see only the achievements, not the difficulties faced and overcome in their pursuit. In *Companions in Courage* I will tell those stories because these folks figure so deeply in my relationship with life's daily issues.

I want you to feel the inspiration and admiration I did, to grab on to that uplifting strength and dignity and turn its power inward. I want adults and children who face challenges and obstacles in their hectic existences to know they're not alone, that others have also fought battles (and worse) and showed they can be won.

These stories speak to the power of the spirit, the soul, the mind, and the heart.

Pat LaFontaine
July 2000

SECTION 1

My
Story

1

My Story

Injuries are part of a professional hockey player's life. I've had several major injuries and many minor ones, but the one that changed my life happened in October 1996 when I was playing with the Buffalo Sabres. It was a major concussion that forced my family and me to put hockey, life, and what really matters into sharper focus.

The game against the Pittsburgh Penguins had barely begun. Skating across the middle of the ice, I was blindsided by a forearm to the head. This shot knocked me out immediately. I flew into the air, lost my helmet, and hit my forehead on the ice. The player who hit me was like a freight train—six foot six, 235 pounds. The only part of my body he hit was my head, but I suffered a second blow when I landed on it.

Here's what my wife, Marybeth, remembers: "The kids and I stayed home that night to watch Pat play. Our six-year-old daughter, Sarah, yelled out, 'Mom, come quick!' I ran to the door of the family room and what I saw froze my heart with fear. Pat was lying facedown on the ice; his body was circling counterclockwise very slowly. I hurried to the phone to call the Marine Midland Arena to check on my husband and was told that he was okay. They said he had a concussion and would probably be back on the ice in two weeks. I had a premonition that the next few weeks, perhaps months, would not be that simple."

I struggled daily against the impact this injury had on my life. An early-childhood memory of falling through the ice and almost drowning kept reoccurring. I grew frantic. I kept grabbing for a "strong piece of ice" and it kept breaking around me. I went under but the water's buoyancy brought me back up. I thought I was going to die. I kept yelling and grabbing, and the ice kept breaking.

And that's the way the next few months unfolded, a nightmare filled with demons and terror. My emotional and spiritual struggles challenged me more than any body-rattling check I had ever received, and our family faced its most severe test.

This concussion left me emotionally drained. My confidence, my courage, and my will to persevere diminished. At times I doubted that I would ever recover. Marybeth had never seen me so depressed, and, on some days, so listless. I could see the fear in her eyes as she watched me flailing, trying to find my balance. The image of me circling, facedown on the ice, haunted her.

The last thing I remember about that injury was waking up. I had been conscious for a good half hour but nothing registered. My conversations with the trainer and my teammates did not stay in my memory. I was in a strange world within myself. I wasn't making sense, and I couldn't make sense out of what had happened to me. I was in our locker room in the lounge area, watching the TV, with my equipment on, disoriented and wondering how I got there. I was wondering why I was in the lounge while a game was going on. Our trainer, Rip Simonick, came into the room because he heard someone talking, but I was the only one in there. He told me that I wasn't making sense.

At that point our team doctor began asking me questions. I started coming to some awareness of what had happened, realizing the medical team would not let me go back on the ice. As I look back today, I have a much greater understanding of the devastating effects of a grade-three concussion.

I saw the neurologist the next day and went through an MRI. The tests were negative, and the docs cleared me to go back and skate just four days after the concussion. Still feeling somewhat groggy and less than 100 percent, I worked hard to convince myself that this concussion wasn't as bad as my previous ones.

Just a week later, I played against Montreal. I remember skating during the warmup and seeing stars and beams of little light particles and feeling tentative. I wasn't myself. I felt very strange and scared and wondered out loud to myself what I was doing out there.

The doctors said I was fine and that I should be able to play. I had been taught that to be a successful hockey player I had to overcome, move forward, and push through the pain. My body was obviously giving me small hints that something wasn't right; however, I was determined to make it right. I was going to push through it and eventually everything would be okay. That's the way it always was for me.

But not this time. Something was wrong, seriously wrong. People were coming up to me and saying, "You know, you look really pale. Is everything okay?" According to my family, I was acting very differently. I still had a constant headache. I continued to be in serious denial, telling myself that I was fine and I would feel better soon if I just pushed through these headaches. I even went so far as to tell myself that this was nothing but a fear of getting hit again.

My frustration heightened when I couldn't sleep at night. I was trying to hide my struggle from my family and the team but I couldn't even get the rest I needed. And I couldn't sleep in the afternoon. I would lie there questioning what was wrong with me. My thoughts were all over the place, so I tried to stop thinking. But I couldn't. During the late nights, my golden retriever, Fred, was my only companion. He had an amazing sense of things not being right. He would follow me everywhere, always by my side, as if he were looking out for me.

I'll never forget what happened after a game in Philadelphia. I tried to hold things together, but my personal struggles, the responsibility of being team captain, and the doctor telling me that I was okay all weighed upon me. I had lost weight and looked pale. During the game, things got really bad. I don't remember a lot, but I felt like I was playing in slow motion. I had trouble taking passes and I felt lightheaded during face-offs. I knew in my heart that I shouldn't be out there. I had no drive or enthusiasm.

We lost the game against the Flyers, and that night I stood in front of my teammates and confessed that I didn't know what was wrong. I told them what they already knew—that I wasn't playing well. The emotions boiled within me as I confessed how bad I felt. I acknowledged that I wasn't holding up my end of the bargain and it was my responsibility as captain to play better and help the team. I felt very strange. Ironically, the first person I saw after leaving the locker room that evening was my close friend and agent, Don Meehan, who immediately saw the distress on my face and, likewise, I saw the concern on his. He could tell I was in trouble.

Here I was, playing a game I loved, and yet I felt trapped, troubled, and confused. The next day I went to practice and sat down with my coach, Ted Nolan. I looked at him for a long time, trying to compose myself, then I told him something was wrong and that I didn't have the enthusiasm and drive of a professional athlete and a captain. When I admitted how scared I felt, I broke down emotionally. I totally lost it. All the heartache of my struggle came pouring out. "Something's wrong with me," I said. He looked at me and told me that I needed help. What a sense of relief that simple observation gave me.

Teddy told me that I was either burned out or in need of some other type of treatment. Then he went to bat for me, telling everybody that I needed to take time off. I was fortunate to have Teddy Nolan for a coach. He cared about me as a player but also as a person. I'll never forget how he supported me.

I'd love to tell you that everything improved after that meeting, but instead it got a little more confusing. I went to see a neurologist and I remember telling him I was very emotional and depressed, totally exhausted and wiped out. I told him that my head was always pounding, that I felt like I was in slow motion and I was scared. That I was not myself.

I'll never forget the doctor looking at me and saying, "Well, listen, you're captain of the team, you're a father of three, and you've just come off a World Cup championship. It's an emotional letdown and a change. Your team isn't doing well and you haven't played as well as you'd like. I'm sure if you throw all of what you are experiencing in a soup bowl, mix it and stir it up, it's no wonder you feel the way you do."

I couldn't believe what I was hearing. Then he told me, "You know, I'm sure if you go out and score a couple goals you'll feel better and everything will be fine."

I remember looking at him and, very emotionally, saying, "Doc, I don't care about scoring goals. I don't care anymore. I'm scared. Something's not right." He responded by saying, "I'm sure everything's going to be fine. Maybe you just need a few days to get some rest."

He didn't understand. For me to say I wasn't interested or concerned about scoring goals or contributing to helping the team win should have been a red flag. At that point, whatever enthusiasm and drive I had left was ripped right out of me. I remember walking around for a while and then going home and telling Marybeth of my concerns as the threads of my life kept pulling loose, unraveling.

I remember trying to read a story to my two daughters. We were sitting in bed and I was trying to keep my focus and concentration on reading that story. I started to skip words. I went back and tried to say the words again. I was ahead of myself and didn't comprehend the story. I was focusing on just trying to read the words right and getting very concerned when I couldn't. Finally I put the book down and told the girls I was sorry but I didn't feel like reading.

It became difficult for me to leave the house or even go from room to room. I felt inwardly terrified. I couldn't watch hockey. I would just glimpse the score. Two or three weeks after my concussion, I watched my first hockey game and couldn't keep up with the play. I sat there wondering how those guys could play. Everything seemed to be happening so fast around me while I was in a punch-drunk state.

Finally, at the Mayo Clinic, two doctors—Dr. Petersen and Dr. Malec—were able to give me the help I needed. They told me that my symptoms were very common in anyone who has had head injuries, vascular damage, or multiple concussions. I remember one of them saying it was as if someone had ripped all your enthusiasm and zest out of you. The tears in my eyes at that moment came from the joy of knowing that someone finally, really, truly understood. The response of the medical personnel in Buffalo to my concussion showed an alarming ignorance of the consequences of multiple head injuries. The following year the club did institute a baseline testing program for every member of the team.

Hopefully my experience has raised the consciousness of the medical profession and professional sports personnel to the seriousness of head injuries.

After my visit to the Mayo Clinic, I found out that what I am describing was all pretty normal for somebody who goes through a head injury. The doctors there told me that the frontal lobe of the brain, where I hit my head on the ice with no helmet, is responsible for one's personality and moods. I had hit the ice without anything breaking my fall. When the medical team at Mayo reviewed the medical history of my head injuries, they pointed out that I was feeling the cumulative effects of my fifth and sixth concussions. Because I had suffered three of them within a year or two, my reserve was so low that I wasn't able to bounce back quickly. They explained that, in my circumstance, it takes much longer to recover because of post-concussion syndrome. For a good five months I battled emotional and depressive issues associated with post-concussion syndrome. It was during this time that I hooked up with Dr. Ernie Valutis, a psychologist, who helped me get through my dark days.

Through my conversations with Dr. Valutis I was able to revisit a number of psychological issues—not just the immediate physical concerns with my concussions, but to work through a number of emotional concerns that were awakened by these injuries. It took a tremendous amount of physical and emotional strength to confront these issues. But I had no choice. I had to deal with them if I was going to get better.

Looking back, I not only had to suffer and work through the physical part of my recovery, but I was surprised at just how much effort I had to put in to work through the emotional hurdles of the post-concussion syndrome.

Healing eventually came. I had neither lost my mind nor my will to compete. I had an injury—an injury as real as

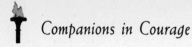

a broken arm or a torn-up knee—but an injury no one could see or lay their hands on.

I had to understand how hurt I was before I could ever get better.

But my journey was not ending. It was just beginning.

2

Beneath the Ice

I fulfilled my dream of playing in the NHL, but dreams and reality don't always fit smoothly together. Having "been there and done that," I understand more about the complexity of living. I am more aware of what truly matters and what we can do to keep ourselves on track regardless of the jarring shots life lays on us.

Many times I have hit the ice. Many times I have fallen. And I question why bad things must happen. Despite the support I've had, life teaches in ways subtle and brutal, and none of us can escape the experience of learning. This realization occurs later to some, earlier to others. It first came to me at a very young age.

My family and I moved to Michigan when I was seven. It was a perfect setting. We lived on Williams Lake, about a mile from the Lakeland Arena. We had a choice—we could skate indoors or outdoors. My brother, sister, and I, along with our friends, found every excuse we could to skate and play hockey.

Hockey was a family affair at our house and always had been. When we were living in Kirkwood, Missouri, my dad, brother, and I would get up at 5:00 A.M. every Saturday and

11

Sunday and skate free until about 7:00 A.M., when the folks who had rented the ice would show up.

The McCoy family would arrive about the same time on the weekends and Mr. McCoy and my dad would resurface the ice before we skated. Mr. McCoy had three sons, so our family would play theirs in shinny hockey—a fun hockey scrimmage. I played shinny hockey until I was about seven, and by then I was hooked. I loved the game and couldn't get enough of it.

My dad had started coaching hockey in St. Louis, and my brother, John, played on his team. I begged to play but I was still too young. Near the end of that school year my dad, who worked for the Chrysler Corporation, was transferred to Michigan. Fortunately for my brother, sister, and me, my parents bought a house on a lake with an ice arena just a mile away. They had hockey programs at the arena, and, at the beginning of the next school year, I started playing for Richardson's Farm Dairy.

I played for Richardson's for two weeks and then I got the break I was hoping for. I was able to join my brother's team. It was more competitive and it also made the travel easier on my parents. Playing at the Lakeland Arena and skating every chance I got out on Williams Lake consumed me. My brother and I, along with our friends, spent hours and hours on the lake.

Preparing the surface of the lake in front of the family home was always a high priority for my dad, John La-Fontaine. At night my brother and I and some of the neighborhood kids would help him clear away any snow that had fallen, smooth any rough spots, and spray a thin layer of water on it in preparation for the next day's activity. Sometimes at night we would hear the lake cracking as the cold air and warm water underneath the ice met. I can remember that Mom would worry about us and not want us to be out there late on weekend nights. She would turn off the lights on the rink as a sign for us to come in. Sometimes we would wait for her to go to sleep, then we'd sneak back in and turn the lights back on and go at it some more. We knew that we would have to repair it in the morning or after school.

Some mornings the surface would be perfect for skating. Other mornings there would be cracks of all sizes in the ice. My dad and I would carefully fill in the cracks with snow and spray water over them so the surface would be good for skating. Cracks made the next day's "skate" a challenge.

From November through March, Williams Lake hosted many contests between the LaFontaine kids, including my baby sister, Rene, and any kid who wanted to play hockey, race, or just skate for the fun of it. My dad taught my brother, me, and the other kids all he knew about skating and the game of hockey. Taking face-offs, learning the proper shooting techniques, skating forward, backward, and in every direction, keeping the head up, and learning to pass the puck were daily lessons taught and learned.

That and, of course, so much more.

About three years after we moved to this lakeside setting, my best buddy, Donny Smith, and I decided to see how far out we could go. We were fearless and the lake was frozen, so we took off.

We got quite a ways out, about a hundred feet, when we heard the ice begin to break under our feet. Donny and I looked at each other nervously, but neither of us wanted to be a "chicken" so we laughed it off and kept walking. The cracking sound got louder. Donny stood there for a moment but I kept going. I got about twenty feet past Donny when the ice gave way and I fell into the frigid water. I struggled to keep my head above the surface and finally caught the edge of the ice with my arms and kept from going completely under. As the ice kept breaking around me, I started yelling to Donny, "Help! Help! Donny! Get my mom!"

Donny, paralyzed by fear, didn't know what to do. Fortunately, as the ice kept breaking around me, I could continue to adjust my grip and keep my head from slipping under, even as the rest of my body flailed away under the ice. My arms were getting numb, but finally I found a strong enough piece of ice. I was exhausted but, calling on all my strength, I pulled myself onto the surface. I lay there for a minute, afraid to move. Finally we crawled off the lake and made our way back to my house. We were both terrified and cold, but when we started to talk about what happened, the fear subsided and we were ready to take on our next adventure.

What amazes me about this story is its simplicity. It is as though I were saying, "I fell through the ice. I got out. My friend was there to help and everything was all right. Life is simple. There's no sweat." I had learned to ignore the dark side.

Unfortunately, I couldn't always avoid the dark side of life.

Why someone close to me had to die at such a young age confused and angered me.

John Brown and I worked together in shop class at Mason Junior High School. I really liked John—he was the tailback on our football team, a regular, quiet-type guy who was everyone's friend. We built birdhouses, shelves, and the kinds of things boys put together in shop.

On a Monday in October I went to class as usual looking forward to seeing and working with John, but he never showed. Afterward I asked what had happened and was told by the teacher that John had broken his tailbone. The whole school was shook up because John, along with Joe Cook, was the reason our football team was so good. We figured our season was down the dumper but next year we'd be on top again because John would be back.

John never came back. John never played football again. He had cancer in the marrow of his bones and that's why his tailbone gave way. Six weeks later, John was dead. I cried myself to sleep for two weeks. I never got to say good-bye to him.

I was shattered. How could such a tragic death happen to my friend? Why did death come? What is death? What does it mean to die? As these questions whirled around inside my head, my mind tried to fit death into my picture of what life was all about. I knew old people died, but why a young person who has had no chance to live? All of us who knew him cried and tried our best to make sense out of his loss.

The rest of that school year was tough, and shop was never the same. One of the things that did help me was just skating on the lake in front of our house. I would talk to John while gliding along on the ice. I don't know if he heard me, but I prayed that he did.

I now realize the confusion young kids feel at difficult times. I know how attitudes are formed based on how we experience life and death. Also, I have come to realize that our youthful perceptions are not always the ones that serve us later in life. Keeping busy, running, not taking the time to deal with the reality of life just doesn't work. Little did I know that falling through the ice, overcoming asthma, and losing a friend to cancer were childhood experiences that would lay a foundation to help me understand life's darker places.

It isn't always trauma that banishes us to those black realms. Sometimes it's success. So much of my life had been governed by the expectations of others. Deep within myself, I knew I could not speak and act on what I really felt in my heart because that would throw the established system out of order. Blessed with athletic talent, I had accomplishments and glory and that overrode my emotional isolation. This entrenched system confronted me squarely when I began to move beneath the surface of my life.

Why look beyond or beneath that surface? I guess we really need to if we're to move forward. Understanding comes hard. But beneath the surface lie the depths.

For me, ice has a certain symbolism. Ice is nothing but water, right? Just frozen water. As a kid skating with his friends, as a hockey player, I put my faith in the ice—that it wouldn't give way underneath me or catch my skate. But the ice can crack and the frigid water that waits below is deadly.

Hockey moves at an accelerated pace, thanks to the ice. With smooth, powerful, gliding strokes, we hurtle toward the goal, seemingly in control. It's an illusion. Control is a momentary blip in a general scheme of chaos. We're handling the puck, trying to evade defensemen poking at it or checking us into the boards. It's like life, only faster. We try to understand it as best as we can as the action whizzes on around us. And, on occasion, we get dumped hard and hit the ice. Ice lacks a forgiving texture. You land and you hurt.

What's next is up to you. You can get up and skate your shift, or you can lie where you've fallen, the chill creeping into your bones. The problem with not getting up is that it gets easier and easier, becomes another way to avoid the challenges and keeps you from accomplishing anything. So you get up. Even when everything aches. You get up and you skate and you finish your shift.

That's simple. That's life. But life, of course, is never that simple.

3

The Evolution of Companions in Courage

Just a few weeks into the 1993 season, when I was playing with Buffalo, I had reconstructive knee surgery and began a long, grueling recovery. Prior to my knee injury I had missed a week here and a month there for minor problems, but never had I sat out a whole season. I was discouraged and angry. I had just ended an MVP-type season, scoring 148 points, and didn't understand the reason for this setback.

It was never my style to sit around and indulge in self-pity, so I tried to keep my attitude up. My message to myself was, "Don't sit there so long feeling sorry for yourself that you don't start learning from what is happening to you."

I thought of the many people who had supported and cared for me in my recoveries. I wanted to give some of that care back to people who were struggling. One day my brother, John, was telling me about some of the kids at his hockey school and he mentioned one of them had a brother undergoing treatment at the Roswell Park Cancer Institute.

My mind drifted back to when I played for the New York Islanders and I got to know a young boy named Clinton Brown.

Clinton suffered from a type of dwarfism that twisted and distorted his bones. He would never grow to be taller than three feet. He had gone through almost thirty surgeries and always seemed to be in a brace. His mom brought him to our practices because he loved hockey. He was our team's inspiration. I knew that many people—many, many people—had been there for Clinton during his trials.

I took this conversation with my brother as an omen, a sign to begin to act on my desire to help others, and much of it began with Clinton. I always remember him as upbeat and enthusiastic, always positive, with a smile on his face. You think attitudes don't matter? Clinton today is nineteen years old and a student at Hofstra University on Long Island, majoring in business finance. He gets around by himself, driving a specially outfitted van. He wants to be a stockbroker and I know he'll be a success. How do I know? Because of what he's been through.

Anyway, after nearly two months of rehab, I went to Roswell Park to meet young Robert Schwegler. He and the other kids made an immediate emotional impact on me. They were in big trouble, yet they were affectionate, hopeful, and giving. We're not talking a broken arm or knee surgery—we're talking flat-out survival. These visits with Robert and other challenged children changed my life. The children I met became my heroes, my first Companions in Courage. They taught me the meaning of courage and inspired and equipped me to face the sort of adversity that life often brings.

Up to this point I had lived my life maintaining a public image as a professional athlete, but my hardship and being a part of young kids' battles pushed me out of my comfort zone and helped me begin to understand life differently. One of my favorite quotes took on new meaning: "To know and not to do is never to know at all."

Hockey is a demanding sport, but its importance is small compared to a child's struggle to live. The pain of a slashing stick, the elbow of an enforcer, or the face-to-face encounters on the ice pale in the light of the physical affliction and devastating impact of cancer. The cancer ward at Children's Hospital and Roswell Park became a different kind of "rink" for me. This time, as a spectator, I watched young children fight a disease in order to win life. I watched them face off in a struggle full of unfair odds. I watched their "coaches" and "general managers"—those caring doctors and nurses—implement a game plan to keep the opposition from scoring. They calculated a strategy using love, support, chemotherapy, medication, and radiation to help their team of courageous kids win their battles.

As I looked on, I learned to love these children. I ached with them, was warmed by their smiling charm, and grieved when they lost their brave battles.

Robert Schwegler and I developed a special bond because he loved hockey. Robert was twelve and had leukemia, a malignant disease in the tissues of the bone marrow. His life was in jeopardy. We spent more and more time together; we played Sega and talked about hockey. Finally, I spoke to the doctors about his love of hockey and wondered how we could get him to a game. While they understood, they were careful to point out that his weight loss and fragile condition would make such a trip dangerous. Protection during transportation and a mask for immunity against the normal spectator environment had to be considered. The cold weather and the general inability to control the people around Robert made it all but impossible.

But something had to be done. My desire to get Robert to a game would not be turned aside. And ultimately the wonderful cooperation of the medical staff made it possible. Since I wasn't ready to return to the ice, I was in the broadcast booth, doing the color commentary. I looked toward section 107 where their seats were located and I spotted Robert's father carrying him. Robert's body looked frail, cradled as it was against his dad. He wore a surgical mask. I watched them settle into their seats and, throughout the game, stole long looks at them, admiring the love between this father and son. They were thrilled to be at an athletic event together. The action of the game was intense, and at one point the announcer turned to me for comment when a puck zipped into the net, but I held up my hand. I couldn't talk. Emotion coursed through me. I was overwhelmed by the thought of Robert and his dad sharing the excitement of the game together.

Later, driving home from one of my visits with Robert, it occurred to me that we could designate a private box at The Aud, the Sabres' former home, just for sick kids. We could provide a private, safe place for kids and their parents. They could enjoy time together with family and experience the excitement of a Sabres game. My first step: Purchase and design a box that would meet these needs.

With the help of my agent, Donnie Meehan, Kenny Martin, the Sabres' director of community relations, and Deidre Daniels, the box soon became a reality.

Robert continued to be an inspiration to me. My family and I were making plans to go to our summer retreat when I got a call from him. He wanted to share some news: On a vacation trip to San Diego he had gone fishing and caught the biggest fish. So before we left on our trip, I went to Robert's house and watched a video of his feat. I told him that he may have reeled in the biggest fish on the West Coast, but I was going to catch the biggest fish on the East Coast.

The evening before we were going to go fishing, my family and I were watching a movie when the phone rang. It was Robert's father. Robert had died earlier that day. I hung up the phone, silently and sadly, and sat for a moment, praying for his family and saying good-bye to my companion. I thanked him for the contribution his short and fragile life had made to mine and my family's. In that moment I realized how close we had become.

The next day, I caught a huge striped bass. I knew Robert was with me. And even today the picture of that bass hangs in our summer retreat and reminds me of Robert and what a wonderful friend he was and continues to be. His happy spirit and the determination he showed in fighting a deadly disease still sustains me when I feel down.

His death stung me, but while I was thinking about Robert, it occurred to me that physical death is not the end of a person. Robert continues to live in my heart and in the hearts of all the people he touched.

In my work with challenged children in hospital wards I have felt life's joys and sorrows. I have learned that we are all companions learning to be courageous, learning to transcend and overcome life's obstacles in order to live out our unique story. I am grateful to all the children who touched my life. They are truly my Companions in Courage and the inspiring co-authors of this book.

4

The Dreams of Youth

P. J. Osika and I were good friends. We were twelve years old and we loved competing against each other. But when we both signed up to run in a summer track meet, I would learn about more than sprinting. Even though P. J. was a runner I figured I could give him a race or maybe even beat him. When we got to the starting blocks for the 220-yard dash, my heart was doing its normal racing before a competition, but I couldn't believe how much I was struggling to catch my breath. The starter's gun cracked and we took off.

For the first hundred yards I was out in front, then I started to gasp for air. P. J. won. I barely made it across the finish line before collapsing on the track. P. J., the other competitors, and the coach ran over and saw that I couldn't breathe. It didn't take long for the ambulance to get there and rush me to the hospital.

About halfway there I started to feel better. They gave me a shot of adrenaline and told me that my mom would meet me in the emergency room. The doctor examined me thoroughly and then delivered the news to me and my mom: I had exercise-induced asthma. I'll never forget his words: "Well, Pat, you might as well hit the books. Your athletic days are over."

I loved sports, particularly hockey. Now this doctor was telling me that I'd never participate in competitive sports again. I remember saying over and over again, "Oh no! No! No! This can't be." And I remember my parents talking to me and telling me, "Things happen for a reason." But right then I could not see the reason, nor did I want to.

I spent that whole summer watching my friends compete in track, baseball, and basketball. I was depressed and lethargic. Every time I exerted myself I started to wheeze, so I watched and hung around the rink and the summer parks. It damn near killed me. I was living a nightmare for a twelve-year-old kid.

My dad and mom began talking to me about courage and perseverance, so I tried my best to suck it up, but I couldn't imagine not playing sports, particularly skating and hockey. Learn to love books and reading more than I loved sports? No way! I couldn't imagine how I would be accepted. I knew that my friendships would have to change because they were based on the acceptance an athlete gets.

The summer was about over when someone suggested to my parents that I see an allergist. Before school started I went to the doctor, took a battery of tests, and found out that I was allergic to just about everything—grass, pollen, mold, ragweed, dust, a variety of foods. The doctor started me on allergy shots and I was back in action before the school year began.

I felt like I had my life back. My whole identity as a young person had been wrapped up in sports and competing. I didn't know any other way. I felt grateful to be back with my friends as "myself" again, doing what I loved to do.

Mike Vaughn and I used to dream together as kids. We talked a lot about what we hoped would happen to us. I used to dream about owning a go-cart, which I thought was the neatest thing, and playing hockey at either Michigan or Michigan State. I worked on my paper route, caddied at the local country club during the summer, and was a rink rat at the Lakeland Arena during the winter. I hoped to make enough money to buy a go-cart and to eventually play college hockey.

My dad would drop my brother and me off and we would caddie for the day. We did that for about five years between the ages of eleven and sixteen. After caddying I delivered my newspapers. When golf season ended, I would work at the Lakeland Arena. I sharpened skates in the pro shop, sold equipment, and swept out locker rooms at the rink. I was a true rink rat. We were always around the rink trying to get extra ice time.

Mike Vaughn was about two or three years older than me. One day I told Mike my dream—how I hoped to get a college scholarship and that one day I wouldn't be sharpening skates and selling equipment, I would be playing hockey at the University of Michigan or Michigan State. We talked about how dreams are achieved and how they come true. We talked about success and individual differences and how important it was for us to be true to our dreams and ourselves.

Another time Mike and I were at the rink and I was sharpening a pair of skates while he worked on a goaltender's glove. He was repairing it, stitching it up and getting it ready to use, when out of the blue he said to me, "Pat, you want to play hockey but I would love to own my own company and make my own hockey equipment."

At the time, Mike was a goalie. He loved playing goal and he loved to work on his equipment to make it better. I said, "Yeah, sure, Mike. And I'll be a professional hockey player." Well, we laughed, thought nothing of it, but both of us, in our own way, kept dreaming and talking about our dreams.

After that last year at Lakeland Arena, Mike and I lost contact with each other. I turned sixteen and he went off to college. Well, my dream came true—I went on to play professional hockey. One day, as I was getting ready to take the ice with the New York Islanders, I noticed the name Vaughn on a goaltender's pads and gloves that were on the floor across from my cubicle. I thought, "Nah, it can't be the same Vaughn, my friend who said he was going to have his own equipment company."

I flashed back to the dreams and talks Mike and I had as young hockey players. I had been realizing my dream for a year and a half as a New York Islander. Could it be that Mike was fulfilling his dream as well?

After the game, I began to inquire about the Vaughn equipment. I was told that the company specialized in goaltending equipment and it was based in Michigan. I asked who the president of the company was. The voice on the other end of the phone said, "My name is Mike Vaughn."

I couldn't believe it. I told Mike who was calling and we laughed and reminisced. To this day, he runs one of the best hockey equipment companies out there. He has branched out into players' equipment.

Mike and I helped each other imagine the kinds of futures we wanted. We didn't know if we'd ultimately get to where we wanted to be, but we set our goals and made up our minds to achieve them. It truly doesn't hurt to dream.

SECTION 2

A Mother's Love

5

Dawn Anna

Throughout my career I've had many coaches, and every one of them passed along something valuable. But I learned the most from my dad, John LaFontaine. He coached me on the lake in front of our house in Michigan, he coached me in bantam hockey, and he has coached and advised me at every level at which I have competed. I'm indebted to my dad for what he taught me on and off the ice.

The relationship between an athlete and his coach is special, particularly when the coach is your father. Our relationship continues to be a source of strength and encouragement. There's a bond built through and around the sport but encompassing so much more and running so much deeper.

It is what helps me appreciate this next story.

About a year ago I was watching the ARETE Awards, given to those who have shown courage in life and athletic competition. A volleyball coach from Columbine High School in Littleton, Colorado, was being honored for her personal and professional courage. I had heard of Dave Sanders, the coach from the same school who gave his life saving kids during that terrible tragedy, but I had never heard of Dawn Anna. When she came to the podium to receive her award, she was accompanied by three of her children. I wondered where her youngest daughter was, because the person who introduced her mentioned that she had four kids. I was stunned to learn that her daughter Lauren was one of the kids who had been shot to death.

I sat in hushed silence, tears welling up in my eyes, as she received her recognition. I thought of my three children, Sarah, Brianna, and Daniel, and how unimaginable it would be for Marybeth and me to lose one of them. I thought of my relationship with my father and mother and what it would be like for us to lose one another. My admiration for this diminutive woman of courage soared when she stood to speak.

I learned that this mother of four had a cerebral malfunction in her brain and had narrowly escaped death herself during two surgeries. I learned that she had coached her team during one period of her life with an IV bag dripping medication and nutrients into her traumatized body. I learned that there were days when getting out of bed to face her day was challenge enough because she could hardly gain her equilibrium, let alone keep her food down.

Then she spoke of April 20, 1999, a day we all remember for its fear and sickening horror. A day when she learned that her daughter, the captain of her volleyball team and Columbine valedictorian with a perfect 4.0 grade average, had been killed while studying in the library. Most of us only saw the terrible spectacle on television; Dawn Anna lives with the results of that massacre and shares that excruciating pain. I couldn't believe what I was hearing.

When Dawn was pregnant with Lauren, she had to fight valiantly to bring her into the world. Twice the doctors thought she had miscarried. During the delivery the hemorrhaging in Dawn's body threatened Lauren's fetal existence. With Dawn's great determination they both survived.

In 1993 doctors found a twisted mass of blood vessels in

Dawn's cerebellum. She battled massive bleeding in order to stay alive. Because of the nature of her surgery, she had to learn to walk again. Her kids, primarily Lauren, taught her as she had taught them. Instead of "Come to Mommy," it was "Mommy, come to me."

They were a team, giving support, encouragement, and understanding. Dawn did learn to walk. She couldn't know she would lose her youngest daughter and once more have to find a way to learn to live.

Now Dawn Anna fights to make libraries safe for kids who want to study. Her daughter became the inspiration for helping kids to make the most of their lives and their potential. A college scholarship has been established and will be given to a Columbine student each year. It is not Lauren's death but Lauren's life that has become her mother's rallying cry as she seeks a way to control the use of guns so that kids can walk the halls of their schools without fearing for their safety.

Dawn Anna's courage touches me each day as I take my kids to school, play games with them, and tuck them into bed at night. Marybeth and I thank God each day for the gift to us that is their precious lives. We also thank God for coaches and parents like my father and Dawn Anna who don't confuse "hard times" with "bad times" by letting their circumstances bury their loving, tenacious spirit.

Dawn Anna is the toughest, most courageous coach I've ever listened to. She knows about winning. She understands loss.

6

Joey Simonick

The wonderful, inspirational time I spent with the kids at Children's Hospital during my playing days in Buffalo are the motivation behind my desire to share the rich stories of so many Companions in Courage. My heart was touched so many times, and each time it was the result of God's little children expressing mature and adult perceptions about life and death. But no list of heroes would be complete without including the parents and other caretakers, who must find a balance between medical facts and the power of the human spirit.

Where do they find this strength, this reserve of grace and will? When I first heard about seven-year-old Joey Simonick, I really wondered about the source of his family's courage. Was it already available to him to draw upon at six weeks old, when his tiny body endured the trauma of an organ transplant? Did it grow and strengthen from its roots in the love and support of Tracy and Joe, his mom and dad, and shape Joey's attitude about life? Was it confidence in the skill of the doctors and nurses who perform the countless mini-miracles that, through transplants, yield new life? Is it, perhaps, in all of us, hidden but available for when we need to tap this deep reservoir to overcome life's obstacles?

As expectant parents, Tracy and Joe Simonick waited for the day of their baby's birth with the usual aspirations and plans and the same worries as any other couple. Parents-to-be always joke about counting fingers and toes, but that nervous jest belies an anxiety. On December 28, 1992, little Joey arrived at Children's Hospital and joy and excitement washed away in a tide of devastation. Two words—"birth defect"—and lives are changed forever.

"We were in shock," Tracy says as she remembers the conference with the medical staff. "Joey and I were told immediately by the cardiologists and cardiac surgeons that little Joey was born without a left ventricle to push the blood to the rest of his body."

The condition, known as hypoplastic left heart syndrome, results in reduced blood circulation due to the absence of the ventricle. This left little time for cuddling and bonding with their newborn; decisions that would affect the quality and duration of a baby's life eclipsed any happy talk. Instead of pleasure, the parents faced unending pressure.

I know the anxious feelings Marybeth and I experience when one of our kids is sick. The mind can wander to so many "what ifs" and unpleasant possibilities. Fear can grow and confusion take charge. So I can hardly contemplate Tracy and Joe's struggles with the choices they had to make.

The doctor laid out the road map for the anxious couple. They could do nothing and simply let Joey's body fail. They could try surgery, through a series of operations called the Norwood procedure. That program would use what was available of their son's heart and create new channels to bypass the left ventricle and keep blood flowing to the rest of the body. This would save his life, the doctor told them, but leave him fragile and probably disabled. Lastly, they could register and wait for a heart transplant.

Choices. How do people reach deep inside and find a way to do what's right, to save not only their baby's life but his potential for really living?

"We did a lot of crying but we decided to agree to try for a heart transplant and keep the operations as a last option," Tracy says. "Because of the kind of people we are, we wanted Joey to have a good quality of life."

Little baby Joey, just four days old, took up residence at the University of Pittsburgh Medical Center on New Year's Eve. His parents moved into the Ronald McDonald House just across the street. Thus began three months of emotional crests and crashes, a boiling pot of tension, hope, prayer, and fears. Each night the Simonicks fretted about whether their son would survive to the next day and long enough to receive a new heart.

They would arrive at the hospital each morning and stay until the nurses gently shooed them out. "The most painful thing was waking up in the morning and calling the nurses to see if Joey lived through the night," Tracy says. "I just couldn't call. Joe had to do it."

Their visits with little Joey wrung every drop of emotion from them. "Joe would go right down to the intensive care unit to be alone with his son. He would bathe him, change his diaper, and cradle him in his arms and just cry," Tracy says.

Joe never pictured himself as one who let his inner feelings escape. At least he never had before. In the quiet times, when he sat and held his baby boy, he discovered something new. "I'm not one to wear my feelings on my sleeve, but this was different," he says. "In case we lost him, I just wanted to connect as much as I could."

As her husband established these bonds with his son, Tracy found herself relying on the memory of her father. Her dad had died three months before she and John married, but now she found herself asking him to protect his grandson.

The passage of time allowed Tracy and Joe to establish their day-to-day activities as more than ritual. This was their life. Their positive attitude, faith, love for their son, and weekend visits from family elevated their morale. They looked to create an upbeat atmosphere and minimize the daily tension. With the Buffalo Bills in the Super Bowl, the Simonicks would dress Joey in Bills gear while the hospital staff, mostly Steelers fans, countered with their own team's shirts. The fun helped.

As they waited for a heart to become available, Tracy and Joe began to establish mental markers for certain dates. January 14 was the anniversary of her father's death, and they hoped that it would be their lucky day. But it came and went. So they focused on Valentine's Day, which they knew would be perfect for a new heart.

The dates came and raised their hopes, then passed and left them crushed. Then finally the word they had awaited came on February 17, and it mixed someone else's pain with their great hopes. An infant in New Jersey had died and the heart had been donated. Joey was quickly prepared for surgery.

They remember the mixed feelings, the sadness for the parents who had just lost their child. But they could not contain their own ecstasy. The operation was a success.

That's not the end of the story. Stories like these never end. Nor do the battles. Joey continues to suffer from the effects of a suppressed immune system. He faced death at his first birthday.

"Sometimes it seems like the transplant was the easy part," Tracy says. "Being on a respirator for three weeks at one year old and always fearing pneumonia or head injury was more difficult."

But Joey began to grow—in size, strength, and vigor. The

Simonicks laced on his first pair of ice skates when he was eighteen months old, and he soon developed a love for hockey. When he was two, a brother, Trevor, joined the family—born healthy.

Joe won't ever forget Joey's first attempts to glide on the ice, helped along by a walker. "Once again I was full of emotion," he says. "After all the little guy had been through, there he was, skating. I was touched, proud, and so happy."

Fear never went totally away. When Joey fell on the ice and his helmet slipped down and cut him, both parents panicked. But they stopped the bleeding and Joey shrugged it off. His father smiled and thought, "His first hockey scar."

The boy born without enough of a heart has showed nothing but heart ever since. In 1998 he participated in the Transplant Games at Ohio State University, a nation-wide competition that features athletes who are transplant recipients. Joey carried the Team Western New York banner into the stadium and won a bronze medal in swimming.

Today, at seven years old, this perfectly normal second-grader skates with the Buffalo Regals mite-level hockey team. His career has hardly started, but he already has a highlight: a two-goal performance in leading his team to a victory.

Tracy and Joe volunteer with the Children's Hospital cardiology unit and serve in TRIO (Transplant Recipients International Organization) and the National Kidney Foundation. They'll talk to anyone anywhere about what they went through.

They know how much they owe to organ donor programs, and Tracy grows wistful when she thinks about her father's passing. "The donor organization asked about our willingness to make my father's organs available. I was resentful and felt they were insensitive to what we were going through," she says. "Now I understand completely."

7

Chris Zorich

If there is such a thing as a recipe for a troubled life, Chris Zorich had all the ingredients. Start with growing up in a four-room apartment at 81st and Burnham, one of the worst neighborhoods in the South Side of Chicago. Stir in an unwed mother and a disappearing father. Add the seasonings of drugs and gangs, life on public assistance, ridicule by bullies because of a white mother and a black father, and the picture seems bleaker still. Top it all off with a huge dose of poverty. Chris remembers being so hungry he would rummage through Dumpsters for scraps.

"There were times the refrigerator was bare," he says. "Sometimes we had macaroni and cheese for lunch and dinner three days in a row."

Other days they would wait in long lines for their only hot meal. There was a towel stuffed in the front window to keep out the cold. The action outside was continuous, with drug deals, car vandalizing, hookers, and winos always a part of the scene. "The apartment was burglarized six times," he says, "and I once had a loaded gun pointed in my face."

The difference in this mixture of potential disaster was the cook, Chris's mother. Zora Zorich handled the adversity with a deep sense of dignity and love for her son and others. Behind the walls of this barren environment the loving arms and firm hand of an amazing woman of Yugoslavian descent balanced the hate and violence with a special brand of love and encouragement. When Chris was very young she would read to him from Raggedy Ann and Dr. Seuss. Books were everywhere, and she often spoke of her favorite, *The Art of Loving* by Erich Fromm. Although she suffered from diabetes and was too ill to work at a full-time job, Zora committed herself to teaching Chris to do his best and to care for those who were less fortunate. "She was a great neighbor and was always there to help others," he says. "For example, she only had a bike, but she would pick up groceries for the elderly neighbors and distribute them. She was a great neighbor and just a wonderful, caring individual." Chris's childhood was wrapped in her courage and love.

Initially, Chris's mom was adamant about his not playing football. When he entered Chicago Vocational High School, he desperately wanted to try out for the team. Zora remained firm. "She wouldn't sign the consent form," Chris says. "I begged and begged, but she didn't want her baby to get hurt."

In his sophomore year he did the unthinkable—he forged her name and joined the team. When she finally discovered his ploy, "I told her it was midseason and I didn't want to let the team down, so she let me play."

A scholarship took him to the University of Notre Dame, just an hour and forty-five minutes from his home. When Chris arrived on campus, he had to fill out some papers that asked about his family. He wrote, "There's only my mom, and she's the best thing that ever happened."

While at Notre Dame he earned the Lombardi Award for the nation's best lineman. Chris capped his career with an outstanding performance in the 1991 Orange Bowl.

While the 10–9 loss to the University of Colorado was heart-breaking, his ten tackles earned him the NBC Sports Award as the game's outstanding player for the Fighting Irish. "I played the best I ever played," he remembers. "But I didn't know why until I got home."

When he arrived in Chicago to see his mom, she did not respond to his knocks on the door of their apartment. It didn't take much for the 270-pound lineman to break down the door, only to find Zora prone on the floor. "She was just lying there and I knew she was dead. I didn't freak out. I just gave a kiss on the lips and said, 'Bye, Mom.'" He added, "Now she can watch over me as my guardian angel."

Chris went on to play for the Chicago Bears and established himself as a generous and loving force for good in the community. He established the Christopher Zorich Foundation to assist those in need. The programs include Care to Share family food distribution; the Love Grows Here Mother's Day program, which distributes flowers and cosmetics to homeless shelters; and the Zora Zorich Scholarship at Notre Dame. Chris takes kids to sporting events, amusement parks, and even to the opera. He answers the phones and helps make deliveries of groceries to the shelters. Memories drive him, memories of Zora and of something else.

"I remember," he says. "I remember what it was like to not have food."

8

Nick Watroba

Larry Watroba knew the sounds of war and the stink of death. He wanted to forget them, bury them as he had buried so many friends and comrades in arms.

Vietnam. Hey, someone had to go. Larry's job was picking up the wounded and the dead behind enemy lines, the helicopters' *whoop-whoop-whoop* just overhead as he collected what remained of American soldiers.

So the birth of his son after his return to South Buffalo, New York, should have been a good thing, a blessing, an easing in his mind. How horrible that he should pass his fear along to his son when his anguished late-night cries, churning out of the memories of that hellish war, woke the little boy and created so much more pain.

As if pain were in short supply for little Nick and his mother, Sandy.

Excited as she was to be a mom, Sandy couldn't help feeling something wasn't quite right with her baby. She wondered about her son's inability to sleep well. As a registered nurse, she had reason to be skeptical when doctors said Nick was just fussy. Her concern was confirmed when Nick's doctor, Peter Dishek, told her the soft spot on Nick's head was too full and that his head size was off the chart.

After a CT scan, a pediatric neurosurgeon delivered the news: "Your son has communicating hydrocephalus due to a forceps injury during birth. His condition is life-threatening." Sandy almost fainted, and Larry wanted to run.

The doctor carefully outlined their options—insert a shunt in the baby's head to drain excess fluid into his abdomen, or risk letting the body compensate on its own, with the hope that the production of spinal fluid would decrease. He explained that a shunt is a lifetime commitment and usually shortens one's life span. The decision needed to be made soon or Nick could suffer seizures, neurological loss, or death. He finished his assessment by saying, "I don't know of any case where the body has compensated on its own, but I know it can."

The Watrobas were in shock when they left the doctor's office, and they tried mightily to cope. Larry battled an old temptation to drink. Sandy went to church. After lengthy, loud discussions and some prayer, they took a courageous step—no shunt. They decided they would risk Nick's not getting well rather than see him handicapped. It was a tense time, and the pressure sent Larry on flashbacks to 'Nam, gave him nightmares that caused him to wake up screaming.

Sandy comforted Nick back to sleep when his dad's fearsome yells subsided, and in time the youngster became conditioned and slept through the night. Larry began drinking again, his nightmares now including his son. Sandy, sustained by a deep faith, prepared herself to face whatever might happen.

The first few months were agonizing as the doctor and the Watrobas carefully monitored Nick's progress. The option of putting a shunt in his head was still open as long as its size didn't increase. After about a year it became apparent that Nick's body was compensating and his hydrocephalic condition was healing. When Nick was six, Sandy started taking him to the neighborhood rink to skate. Soon, with the doctor's permission, his parents started taking him to Holiday Twin Rinks in Cheektowaga, where he would skate around wearing a helmet and carrying a hockey stick. By age seven Nick was cleared to start playing competitive hockey in the Holiday House League.

At twelve, he started playing golf. Using a set of clubs he found in the trash and balls he fished out of a lake, he won the Junior Summer League tournament and was featured in the *Niagara Golfer,* a local publication. Obviously this kid, who couldn't do anything for the first six years of his life, had athletic talent.

Serendipity helped move Nick's hockey career along. One day he joined a threesome at South Park Golf Course that included John Hillery, a man who sponsors students to attend Timon/Jude High School in South Buffalo, New York. Impressed with Nick's athleticism, Hillery asked if he would like to go to Timon. Nick was thrilled and attended for two years, excelling on the ice and the golf course. In his second year he was voted MVP. When the school's season finished, Watroba played for the Buffalo Regals, coached by Jim Reaume, a man who has encouraged and inspired Nick throughout his young career. Watroba captained the Regals for two years before joining the Depew Saints Select team. His play for Timon, the Regals, and the Saints led to his selection to the Western New York All-Scholastic first team.

The first time the Select team played in Canada, Nick was shocked at the size and speed of some of the Canadian players. In his room after the first game he struggled with whether or not he could compete. He thought about his dad and mom's courage and Coach Reaume's words: "Even if you're small, Nick, use that to your advantage. Play the angles and tap into your inner strength."

Nick distinguished himself and was invited to play in the Prospects Tournament in Sarnia, Canada. He played for the Bluewater Sharks and was selected as one of the top players in the U.S. and Canada. Because of that achievement, he was awarded a scholarship to Kimball Union Academy, a hockey prep school in Meridian, New Hampshire.

I admire the Watroba family for modeling how to love and support one another through their crises—Vietnam, a hydrocephalic diagnosis, alcoholism, and the tension created by that tough combination. Leaving the safe confines of western New York has been a challenge for Nick, but he is ecstatic about playing for Kimball. In his first game, with scouts from Division I and the NHL in attendance, Nick scored two goals and had two assists.

Given the chance to perform a miracle, his body came through. Facing the challenge of pulling apart or pulling together, his family fought to stay intact. Easy? Absolutely not, not for Nick or Sandy or Larry. But worth it? Yes. Oh, yes.

9

Alison Pierce
and Family

She would pull on her skates and scrap with anyone on the ice. The game just meant so much. Alison Pierce loved playing hockey. She excelled in this demanding sport, relished its challenges. And she excelled when life put unreasonable demands on her.

She loved to skate and compete against her younger brothers, Michael and J. T., on Snow Pond near their home in Princeton, Massachusetts. Ali, twelve, with her long black hair, contagious smile, and irreverent sense of humor, shouldn't have had to worry about too much more than chasing down loose pucks. This was childhood, the good times.

Neither she nor her parents were prepared for the news they received just two days before Christmas. On December 23, 1994, Ali embarked on a journey that would test the heart and resolve of a seasoned athlete, let alone a twelve-year-old just beginning her career. She was diagnosed with life-threatening liver cancer.

Together with her parents and her brothers, she was determined to fight this disease with the same high energy and competitive fire that she exemplified on the ice. When she lost her hair, her attitude was, "There is one good thing about chemotherapy. You can never have a bad hair day." And by the end of her chemotherapy, her tumors had shrunk.

What was left of the diseased cells was removed surgically, and Ali returned to the eighth grade the next semester. John and Anna, Ali's parents, had anguished over their daughter's plight, so they were deeply relieved when she was back in school. Her brothers, who missed her competition out on Snow Pond, looked forward to taking her checks again. This young woman had already faced death and could again live with joy and enthusiasm.

One day, when Ali was noticeably quiet, her mom asked her if anything was wrong. "It bothers me that my friends don't understand what life is all about," Ali told her solemnly. "They're upset because some boy won't talk to them or they feel fat. They just don't get it."

Maybe she had already matured beyond her years, gained a wisdom rare even in adults. How many people would say, as she did, "Cancer is the best thing I've ever gone through"? That's a perspective only life's harshest difficulties could mold, and one that gave her parents and brothers the strength to face the wrenching twists that lay ahead for them.

It was only a year later that Christmas again brought an unwelcome visit—Ali's cancer had returned. The Make-A-Wish Foundation offered the family a Hawaiian vacation, but Ali's response was simple: "No. I've traveled. Let someone else have the chance to go."

Over the ensuing months, John and Anna worked desperately to find a remedy for Ali's cancer. And through it all, this young woman hockey player showed the courage of a veteran, maintaining her calm and an aura of peace.

When Anna broke down in tears of grief, Ali comforted her mother. "It's okay," she told her. "What is, is."

So Ali battled cancer. But an indomitable spirit proved no match for a progressive, insidious disease. Alison Pierce died on November 3, 1996, and her devastated family began to consider funeral arrangements.

They found that Ali had made some arrangements of her own. She had asked her friends to wear red to the funeral. To honor her beloved daughter's wishes, Anna went out and bought a red dress. We think of funerals as dark and somber, the black of the mourners reflecting death's emptiness, but red ruled at Ali's funeral. It celebrated the living memory of the vibrant girl who shook life by its lapels, who lived with the same vitality she had shown on the ice.

Parents should never have to bury a child. And they certainly don't feel much like conducting the mundane business of their own lives in the aftermath. It wasn't any different for the Pierces. Anna felt as if she would never stop crying. John could barely manage his brokerage firm, let alone his shattered feelings. Michael and J. T. continued to play hockey, but they always felt as if they were a skater short and their games just didn't seem to matter much.

Thanksgiving came, three weeks after the funeral. Anna went looking for John and found him in Ali's room, weeping and wrapped in memories. As she held him, John told her, "The best day of my life will be when I leave this world and join Ali."

They talked. They hugged. And they agreed they couldn't let grief diminish them, that they needed to be strong parents for their two sons, that they simply had to live in a way that would honor the daughter they'd cherished so.

They kept that promise. They threw their energies into creating the Ali Pierce Endowment Fund through the University of Massachusetts Cancer Center. This fund would support pediatric cancer care and research. John, an ex-marathoner, got his friends and colleagues to secure pledges from their associates to sponsor them in the Boston Marathon. They set a goal—$500,000 in five years. And those who joined them became known as Ali's Army.

Yet they struggled. Anna, who was shy and self-conscious, was still too grief-stricken to take part publicly. When she tried to return to Ali's classroom at Notre Dame Academy to give each girl a red carnation that symbolized Ali's memory, she simply could not. She finally asked the teacher to distribute the flowers. Anna couldn't bring herself to see that roomful of young, lively ladies.

Ali's Army began to prepare for its first Boston Marathon, which would take place about eleven months after Ali's death. John and many of his supporters drove up to Hollis, New Hampshire, to run a half-marathon.

He didn't come back.

As Anna worried where he was, as the starting time for Michael's hockey game neared, the phone rang.

"Mrs. Pierce, I'm sorry but your husband has collapsed," said the caller. "You need to come right away. They are giving him CPR."

Anna gathered the boys together and did her best to give them the news. "Daddy's at the hospital," she said, "but he is strong and he loves you guys very much. He'll be all right."

J. T. told her, "He'll be okay. God would never do two terrible things to us in one year."

And that's when Anna knew. Even as she frantically dialed the hospital, even as the doctor began to speak, she knew.

"We tried everything," he said. "But we were not able to revive your husband."

Ten feet from the finish line, John Pierce had fallen to the ground, the victim of a heart attack.

Anna put her arms around her sons. She told them, "Daddy's gone. He's with Ali."

J. T. screamed and ran away. Mike hugged his mother and then both of them chased down J. T. Anna grabbed him, shook him, screamed louder than he could: "We will make it. We're going to be all right. We are going to make it." Perhaps if she could convince them, she could also persuade herself.

And together, together, they sobbed.

At the hospital, Anna looked at her husband. Fit. Handsome. How could this be? Yet in that moment of the deepest sorrow she had ever felt, she also found that peaceful calm Ali had known and showed.

Lying next to John was his cap, the one with "In Memory of Ali" stitched on it. Anna thought about his words on that Thanksgiving Day. "He's with Ali," she told herself. "How can I not be happy for him and for her?"

Bright sun played off the dying autumn leaves as she awoke the next morning. Somehow there wasn't any question about what to do next, what to do in the weeks and months and years ahead. She had sons to raise, and her own life to live as a tribute now to both Ali and John. She had watched cancer strengthen her daughter, even as it took her from her. She had seen Ali's death transform John and make him live even harder and more selflessly, ultimately giving his life in her cause.

The shy and self-conscious Anna disappeared that day. The new Anna had a mission. She spoke of it at John's funeral, reading from a letter she had written to her departed love: "I will raise our sons to be like you. And I promise you I will carry on the work you have started with Ali's Army. But now we will call it Ali and Dad's Army. My sweet John, thank you for all you have given us."

Anna became the Army's spokesperson. She appeared on the *Today* show. Her aversion to crowds faded. Hockey games, races, fund-raisers, all became venues to tell her story: "I have a daughter named Ali. She left this earth, but she goes on and I continue to celebrate her life."

On Ali's sixteenth birthday, Anna took a bushel of roses to Notre Dame Academy and handed them out, one to each girl in Ali's class. On November 18, 1998, Ali and Dad's Army—all those friends and family members, Ali's former coaches, Michael and J. T.—staged a hockey match against the Boston Bruins alumni team. The proceeds from that game put the Ali Pierce Endowment Fund over its goal of $500,000—in just thirteen months.

When Anna and the boys stood watching the runners warm up for the 1998 Boston Marathon, a reporter asked her how she felt about fulfilling her husband's dream after such terrible pain and tragedy.

She paused before answering. And then she said, "Two years ago, we were a family of five. A year ago, we were a family of four, then a family of three. How blessed we are today to number in the hundreds. No, this is not a tragedy. This is a love story."

SECTION 3

A Father's Strength

10

Rich Morton

When the 1998 high school football season began in Salamanca, New York, coach Rich Morton faced two problems that were disguised as one. It would be enough if he were known only as the guy replacing a local legend and his own mentor, the area dean of coaches George Whitcher. But Rich Morton was also a recovering cancer patient.

Coach Whitcher had led his team to seven sectional titles in twenty-five years, and he wanted to continue coaching after he retired. The school board said no and appointed Morton, who had missed the entire 1997 football season because of his illness. He had gradually regained enough stamina to coach wrestling, but it took him a year before he got his health and endurance back. When he was promoted to head football coach for the 1998–99 season, people openly questioned whether he was strong enough to weather the stress.

But Morton prevailed. Grateful for the opportunity, willing to push himself and carefully guide his players, he led his Salamanca Warriors to a 12-0 record and into the title game against Edgemont High School.

Winning didn't change the other elements in Rich Morton's life. Some things have remained constant and true to this day. Every time he goes to Roswell Park Cancer Institute in Buffalo for a checkup, he leaves grateful for the gift of life. Yes, Rich has had cancer twice. Yes, he goes to Roswell to make sure that his cancer is under control. But he comes away appreciating the blessing of his own life and the indomitable spirit of the people who are fighting for their own.

In the fall of 1999 Rich was at Roswell for his four-month checkup. As he departed, he couldn't help but notice a weary-looking teenage boy about the same age as most of his players at Salamanca. The doctors were drawing his blood and examining his drained body. Morton understood the kid's struggle because he knew firsthand just how much energy cancer saps from the body. When he walked by, he gave the kid the thumbs-up sign; the boy barely smiled.

Driving back to Salamanca, Morton couldn't stop thinking about the young man and the hard path before him. When he met his football team for practice later that afternoon, he felt acutely aware of how healthy his players were compared to the kid he had seen earlier that day. He did not want to hear their complaints about running wind sprints or being tired. He called them together and began telling them about the boy at Roswell. The team, intent on its final preparations for the Class C state title game in Syracuse, listened carefully. Morton asked a question: "What do you guys think that kid would choose—the demand and the soreness from a few conditioning wind sprints or the fatigue from his cancer treatment?" The silence gave him his answer.

Coach Morton, as he always tried to do, used football to teach his team about life. The lesson: "Keep things in perspective, guys. Be grateful for your health. Work hard to become better at everything you do. Don't waste good, positive energy complaining."

The Salamanca Warriors had a spirited practice that

night, in keeping with the emotional high of a title game. The team and everyone in town bubbled with excitement about the championship game to be played in the Syracuse University Carrier Dome. Morton felt that same enthusiasm but found himself oddly pensive too.

He sat alone, reflecting on the last two years. In 1997, Morton wasn't sure he would be alive, let alone a husband, a father to his kids, or a coach to his team. He had survived a bout with testicular cancer in 1991 and thought he was cancer-free until he was jogging one summer morning and had trouble breathing. On July Fourth he went to Roswell to get a checkup.

Three days later Coach Morton was told to come to the hospital immediately. He had a softball-size tumor in his chest. He began chemotherapy the next day.

His wife, Julie, his daughters, Britney and Andrea, and son, Eric, pulled together on a "God Job." They reminded him: "God heaps challenges on you, and he's there to get you through."

Those challenges can seem insurmountable.

"That was a very difficult period in my life, and hopefully I won't have to go through it again," he says. "You don't know if you're going to live or die. You don't know what tomorrow will bring. I wouldn't wish cancer on my worst enemy."

Easy as it is to question fate, Morton instead stuck to a path of healing.

"I don't ask why it happened to me. I just asked for the strength to get me through it. I think that's what's so important about sports, how it can teach kids to deal with things. This year was just another hurdle you have to deal with. We're dealing with kids here, it's important that we teach them about the game of life as well as the game of football."

The Salamanca Warriors played inspired football in 1999.

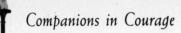

Each opponent reminded the players of the foe their inspiring coach fought each day. His courageous attitude, his hard work, and his understanding of a "God Job" required them to dig deep inside themselves to play up to their potential.

When Coach Morton stood on the sidelines at the Carrier Dome and listened to his daughters sing the national anthem, his heart offered a hymn of gratitude for his life, his family, his team, and his challenges.

Often it is not the end of a journey that is the reward. It is the journey itself that is the blessing.

11

Rick and Dick Hoyt

The captain of the North Reading, Pennsylvania, high school football team married a cheerleader. Sounds like a little bit of the American dream, right? Well, Dick and Judy Hoyt lived a nightmare but persevered to ensure a happy ending.

When their first child, Rick, was born in 1962, they hardly knew what to say or do when they were told he was a nonverbal quadriplegic. They were barely more than kids themselves, neither over twenty, and they'd just been told to institutionalize their son.

"We felt like we were at the bottom of a black hole," Judy says. "Someone had just put a cover over our dreams and snuffed them out."

The couple had known a different life, one of achievement and high standards. They wanted and expected more. So they rejected the doctor's advice and sought counsel from the minister who had married them. He told them that they had another choice—"Keep Rick at home. Love him, take one day at a time, and see where it leads you. Who knows what will happen?"

They took those words to heart, and that decision started an incredible series of events that demonstrate the power

57

of love. Two young parents had a handicapped child, no rules or precedent to guide them, a society that tends to hide folk that don't fit an acceptable standard, shattered dreams, and their future in front of them. When adversity is met with love, commitment, and determination, it brings out the best in us.

When Judy and Dick drove away from the hospital after Rick's birth, Dick cried, one of the few times that has ever happened. Their son needed constant attention. Judy was beside herself at times: "Sometimes I screamed, 'I just can't take care of this child!' One day I was so angry I went into a closet and screamed and cried. There were times I hated Rick."

Some of their friends agreed with the doctor and thought they should put Rick in a home. Some thought he was retarded. Eight months into their parental challenge, Rick was diagnosed with cerebral palsy, and that, oddly enough, was good news. With each day that passed, it was becoming clear to Judy that Rick was not retarded. He could have a life, a real life, and his family would see to it that he did.

Rob, who was born in 1964, and Russ, who was born in 1967, became involved in Rick's care and instruction as they got older. Through the help of Children's Hospital, Judy gradually exposed Rick to the world of sensory perception. She played music, banged on pans, and rubbed his skin with different fabrics. She began teaching him the alphabet by using sandpaper letters glued to blocks. Judy was heartened when she realized that Rick had a sense of humor—he started laughing at her jokes.

While these developments were encouraging, Dick struggled. He seemed to always have a reason to be out of the house. The lion's share of the parenting was Judy's.

When Rick reached school age, the Hoyts faced new challenges but found new friends to help them through. Dr. William Crochetiere of Tufts University and Rick Foulds, a grad student, introduced them to Tufts Interactive Communicator. Through the use of a head switch, Rick could select letters from a panel. The Hoyts called it the Hope Machine. Through innovative fund-raising and the help of their neighbors, the Hoyts were able to bring the TIC home in 1972. They were about to "hear" Rick speak. The family couldn't believe it when he tapped out his first words— "Go Bruins." Boston was in the Stanley Cup finals and Rick was cheering them on. He smiled with delight.

"It marked a time for people outside our family to realize that Rick was intelligent and that I was not just some crazy mother saying, 'My kid is bright,'" Judy says.

Because of Judy's efforts, Rick was able to enter public school in 1975. When he reached his senior year at the age of nineteen, he wrote an essay titled, "What It Is Like to Be a Nonverbal Person." In his writing, Rick let loose his feelings of anger and of being cheated, despite his family's unceasing efforts.

"I felt and knew I was different," he wrote. "I understood all the things said to me. Being a nonverbal person does not make one any less of a human being. I have the same feelings as anyone else. I feel sadness, joy, hunger, love, compassion, and pain."

In 1978 a local college sponsored a five-mile race to raise funds for an injured lacrosse player. Rick asked his dad if he would push him in the race. Dick agreed and they entered the competition. With Dick pushing Rick in his awkward wheelchair, they finished next to last, but their relationship and their joint athletic endeavors were launched.

That night, Rick went to his computer and typed out with his head, "Dad, when I'm out running, I feel like I'm not handicapped." Dick was moved by his son's message. They had a running chair designed and built, and the father-son racing tandem began to train. This breakthrough meant as much or more to Dick as it did to Rick. Formerly aloof, he became more intimately involved in the lives of all three of his sons as he worked more and more with Rick.

In just two years the Hoyts were entering fifty races a year, with Rick and Dick running the races and Judy, Rob, and Russ providing support. Sometimes they would race three times on a weekend. They thrived on the competition and their relationship with each other and their fans grew in number. In the heat of a race, Rick would urge his dad on by moving his arms and legs. Dick says, "I had to tell him to take it easy. You're going to tip the chair over. Rick encourages me if he hears me breathing hard. He turns around and gives me a smile. Rick and I talk together by me just looking at his eyes."

Once, after a mediocre race, Rick wrote on his machine, "Dad's getting old. Maybe it's time for a new pusher."

In 1981 Dick and Rick unofficially entered the Boston Marathon by falling in behind the other wheelchairs. In November of 1982 they officially qualified by posting a time of 2:45 in the Marine Corps Marathon. They have run in practically every Boston Marathon since and have become racing legends in New England. Bill Rodgers, a four-time winner of the Boston Marathon, expressed the sentiments of fans and athletes alike: "It's a world-class effort. Everyone in marathoning is inspired by the Hoyts."

Next came triathlons, believe it or not. One of their ironman efforts stretches the bounds of the imagination. They competed in the Ironman Canada Triathlon Championship, which began at 7 A.M. Eighteen hours later, the Hoyts were still on the course but within a hundred yards of the finish line. They were exhausted!

They had finished the 2.4-mile swim with Dick towing Rick in an inflatable dinghy; they had finished the 112-mile cycling event riding their custom-made bike; now they were nearing the end of the 26.2-mile run. Rick looked back at his dad to encourage him. The applause of the crowd, which was still four deep along the thoroughfare in Penticton, British Columbia, renewed their resolve to finish this grueling test of endurance. They crossed the finish line with "Chariots of Fire" blaring over the PA.

It didn't matter that the race had been won eight hours earlier. People knew the Hoyts were out there, and they wouldn't miss their finish for anything.

Beginning and finishing races on designated courses and in the tight corners of life's uncertain terrain is a Hoyt family trademark. Today Lieutenant Colonel Hoyt, a career officer in the National Guard, feeds, changes, and cradles Rick. He no longer finds reasons to be out of the house. The rest of the Hoyts have also been active. Judy drafted a new Special Education law; she helped form the Association for Human Services; she set up Kamp for Kids and earned a degree in childhood development; and she "womaned" the support van during many of the races. Russ created the "spell method" to improve the speed of the Hope Machine. Rob taught his dad to swim. What a family!

And what is Rick up to? He graduated from Boston University and now works at Boston College, helping design a new computer, Eagle Eyes, that is controlled by eye and head movement. He has completed 780 races with his father, including 55 marathons and 149 triathlons.

Rick's handicap opened doors and pushed the Hoyts through them to achieve beyond their wildest dreams. In Judy's words, "We're not the Brady Bunch. We're not the perfect American family. We're not any different from any other family. We've made what could have been a 'poor me' experience into a positive."

If only we could all be so average.

12

Amp Campbell

Growing up in Sarasota, Florida, Amp Campbell had a dream. Someday he would play big-time college football. Someday he would strap on the pads, buckle the chin strap, and contribute to a nationally ranked team, help it rise to the top. Maybe he would even move on and compete with the professionals in the NFL.

He walked, talked, and breathed football. He listened to his heroes say, "You can do it." He believed it. He practiced it. He played it. Hard work, determination, and never losing sight of his lifelong goals brought him to his freshman year at Michigan State University. In fact, he arrived in 1994 as *Parade* magazine and *USA Today* All America and *Parade*'s top cornerback in the country. He loved defense, and he loved the challenge and hitting that went with being an aggressive cornerback. He proved it by leading Riverview High School to the state quarterfinals and returning twenty-three kicks for touchdowns, a school record.

But life at Michigan State involved more than learning coverages. There were other books as important as the Spartans playbook. Amp realized that a little late, and academic ineligibility tainted his freshman year. Amp blitzed the books, studied, and improved his grades, and for the next two years enjoyed tremendous success with the Spartans. In 1996 he led the team in fumbles caused. His hard-hitting style earned him the Tony Love award for the team's most improved defensive player. In 1997 he was voted all–Big Ten second team.

But this struggle paled against what Campbell would face next. In 1998, just ten minutes into the second game of the season, against the University of Oregon, Amp broke his neck while making a tackle. There was talk of paralysis and odds against his even walking again. Fans in Michigan were both sympathetic and knowledgeable, remembering all too well the story of Mike Utley of the Detroit Lions, who suffered a career-ending and paralyzing injury in a game at the Pontiac Silverdome.

Amp had surgery that fused his sixth and seventh verte-brae with bone and a steel plate. The doctors drilled a pair of holes in his skull and fitted him with a halo brace to lock his head in place. The surgery was successful, but the prognosis was not good. Yet Amp kept and nursed his life-long dreams.

To some, his aspirations seemed to be a simple denial of reality. Could he not see his physical condition, sense its limitations? Amp had different ideas. Even as he struggled to walk, he wanted no part of the whispered fears that he'd never play football again.

His parents, Johnnie and Pearl Campbell, were watching the fateful game on TV in their Florida home. Within min-utes the doctors were on the phone saying their son was lucky to be alive. They said he would recover but his ca-reer was over. Johnnie's memories were all too vivid. He had had a hip replacement at the age of thirty, the result of years of construction work and lifting concrete. He too was disabled. His mother had been his nurse and care-taker—now it was time for him to tend to his son.

He moved into an extra bedroom in Amp's apartment

with Amp's girlfriend, Denise, and daughter, Kiera. He would help Amp dress and tie his shoes. He would feed him spoonful by spoonful, just as he had when Amp was a baby. As Amp's recovery progressed, his dad drove him to his classes. "I would wander into some of the classes and listen. I learned a few things," Johnnie says with a smile. His devotion fed Amp's hope and courage.

Despite the physical pain, Amp often said the real pain was not being able to play with two-year-old Kiera. "When I told her I couldn't pick her up and do the things I normally did with her, she started to cry," Amp says.

Each day Amp faced the enemy within—the urge to give up. Each day he struggled with life's simplest chores. But as he did, he became more convinced he could not allow pessimism to seep in, to take up residence in his thoughts.

He tapped into the same spirit of determination that had brought him this far. Just imagine what it is like for an athlete of his ability to be helped to walk just a few steps at a time. Imagine sleeping with a halo neck brace, instead of a football. Still, Amp took up his rehabilitation program with fierce courage. His playbook now consisted of daily weight lifting, stretches, and mental focus exercises with a new and demanding coach—a physical therapist.

Months and months of commitment paid off. Amp's body grew stronger and his sense of direction more positive.

Nick Saban, who was the Spartans' coach then, tells the story of Amp coming to the dressing room soon after he was able to get around. The team had lost its first two games and Amp wanted to meet with his teammates before the Notre Dame game to encourage them. Seeing his courage and fight was no small part of their victory that day. Saban recalls, "I've never pulled for a player the way I've pulled for Amp. What he has done makes me feel better than beating the 49ers or beating Ohio State last year when they were Number 1. No matter what happens from here, we've won."

They named Amp a captain for the duration of the season of his rehabilitation, a recovery that stretched the bounds of credulity. Later that season, when Amp was in his rehab program, the team wanted him to go out on the field for the coin toss. Amp recalls that his mood was quiet and introspective. He says, "I didn't want to walk out there with them." But when Amp, in his number 3 green jersey, neck brace and all, walked onto the field, applause poured down. Amp's eyes teared up and he remembers, "I felt very emotional. I started crying, listening to our fans build me up that way. I'm real glad I went out there."

They won the toss and the game, and Amp moved one step closer to his own victory.

And then, the very next season, Amp returned. That's right. He returned—ready to play. In the season opener he hoped for an uneventful start, a tackle or two, just the chance to get it in gear again. Against, of all teams, Oregon.

It was tied 17–17. The six-foot 200-pounder, healthy and alert, picked up a fumble and returned it for a touchdown.

Remember how Amp set a high school record by scoring twenty-three touchdowns on returns? This was the best return of all.

13

Joetta Clark Diggs

Again. Joetta Clark felt the desire building within, and she was determined to run the 800 meters at the 1999 Millrose Games again.

That's not so hard to understand. Champions always feel there's one more great race somewhere within them. Joetta Clark first competed in the Olympic trials twenty years ago as a seventeen-year-old, eventually establishing an enviable record as well as a collection of trophies and ribbons. She had competed in three Olympic Games and had won numerous USA Track & Field Indoor and Outdoor titles. By 1998 Joetta had run in twenty Millrose Games at Madison Square Garden and had been the Millrose 800-meter champion six times. Her track career at the University of Tennessee reflected her fifteen All-America honors.

After starting to run at age ten in both the Essex County, New Jersey, camps and playgrounds program and in high school, Joetta first came to prominence with her seventh-place finish at the Olympic trials in 1980. Her father, Joe Clark, the well-known tough high school principal portrayed in the movie *Lean On Me*, directed the youth program, and his influence on Joetta was part of her competitive drive.

"Dad taught us to do the best we could in anything we attempted and to always be prepared," she said.

While her father resists admitting that he downplayed sprinters, Joetta remembers it differently. "Dad thought sprinting was for lazy people. At that time black Americans weren't running distances or cross-country, and he wanted us to say we can do those events." She also remembers that part of Dad's motivation was in his opinion that "long-distance running builds character and those virtues, values, and resolves that will ultimately catapult you from moments of despair to the perfect cadence of success."

Whenever I read about a father's influence on his children through the sharing of the values that he both believed and modeled, I'm encouraged and heartened. When my three kids struggle through their experiences in life, I recognize the vastness of my responsibility. I'm not sure how tough I am, but I read that Joe Clark, who carried a baseball bat through the school halls, sees himself as even tougher than he is depicted in the movie. His take: "I was an unswerving, determined, quixotic crusader."

Well, as uncompromising as he might have been, he certainly influenced Joetta.

By age thirty-six, Joetta had accomplished much, off the track as well as on it. Away from competition, her life continued to center on giving back to others. She founded a company that concentrates on helping corporations develop mentoring programs to assist high school students, and in 1997 she was appointed as a commissioner for the New Jersey Sports and Exposition Authority.

So why the push to run the Millrose in 1999? On September 15, 1998, Joetta's car was demolished by an eighteen-wheeler. She was driving on a New Jersey Turnpike on-ramp when the truck merged into her lane, smashed into her mid-size car, and sent her spinning backward down the highway. Her car rolled and settled some seventy-five yards away. She was trapped and had to be rescued.

"When you're pinned in your car like that and you try to move your leg and you can't...and you try to move your arm and you can't," she recalled, the emotions of being back in that moment rising, "you don't think you'll ever be able to do anything again. I certainly didn't think I would be able to run Millrose."

The damage was severe—a concussion, torn stomach muscles, two torn vertebral disks, and damaged nerves in her left eye. Bedridden for three weeks, she could not tamp down the competitor inside.

"I needed a target," she said. And so this Companion in Courage set her sights on the women's 800-meter race at the 1999 Millrose Games.

She courageously worked through the weakened leg condition and the headaches from the eye injury. She resumed jogging just before Thanksgiving. In January 1999 she visited her brother, J. J., who had coached her in the past, and he told her she would be recovered enough to run Millrose. Why put her body through both rehab and training? She summed it up quickly: "I'm a tough competitor."

And compete she did. When the starter's gun sounded it was a weakened but confident Joetta that shot from the blocks alongside the best in the United States.

"I was scared," she recalled. "I didn't know what to expect, so I just ran aggressively. I wanted to run to show how thankful I am to all the people who helped me. This will be a thank-you to them."

The field was packed with great athletes, and the crowd sensed the significance of the race. Joetta started strong and led for three laps. With all her courage and inner strength, she ran a great race, but her tired body faded near the finish. With most of the field behind her she crossed the line less than half a second behind Meredith Valmon.

Second place? I don't think so. I think Joetta Clark won a bigger race by getting back on the track. She married Ronald Diggs in September 1999 and closed her incredible running career with still more amazing achievements. She won her seventh Millrose 800-meter title in February 2000 and made the 800-meter U.S. delegation in the 2000 Olympics a family affair, finishing third (1:59.49) in the Olympic trials behind her younger sister, Hazel Clark (1:58.97), and her sister-in-law, Jearl Miles-Clark (1:59.12). Joetta finished eighth in the second heat of the semifinals in Sydney. What a competitor. What a Companion.

14

Derek Stingley

I love sports. You would think that as a professional athlete I would tire of the weekly battles on the ice, the court, the field, or the course. I don't. I love the up-close-and-personal stories that make each athlete's life and performance more meaningful. I have always been drawn to a person's story and its effect on and off the field. I am touched by the stories of athletes who give support to one another and the understanding they have of what each of us goes through.

One of the most meaningful pieces of memorabilia hanging in my office is an autographed number 16 jersey of Joe Montana and a football signed by Joe, Dwight Clark, and Jerry Rice. I'll always remember the Montana-to-Clark play, known as "The Catch," that started the San Francisco 49ers on their way to five Super Bowl wins.

During my recovery from an injury with the New York Islanders, Joe Montana understood my physical and mental battle. He autographed and sent the jersey with a letter of encouragement and support. He reinforced my already larger-than-life perception of him as someone who is not only a superstar but a superhero. Joe gives back to others because of his love and understanding of sports.

Another athlete who symbolizes such a giant spirit is Derek Stingley. His athletic ability and drive is built on the spirit of his father, Darryl Stingley. In 1978, as a New England Patriot, Darryl took the kind of violent defensive hit that brings football fans to their feet in appreciation. But this time it was a one-in-a-million shot that quickly hushed the cheers of the crowd to silence and prayer. Darryl was paralyzed for life. Derek was seven years old at the time.

"I was too young to understand what it meant," Derek recalls. "I found out what happened when I saw him for the first time in the hospital. I wanted him to get up and he never got up. That was the hardest thing I had to face as a boy."

As a father, my private thoughts often include the hopes and dreams I have for my kids. I want to be around to love, support, and be a part of their journey. Darryl was no different. When he allows himself to revisit the injury and his fears of the moment, he says, "At that time Derek was a very young kid and I thought to myself, 'What would happen to him?' I remember just going into prayer and asking God if he would spare my life and allow me to see my sons and their families grow."

He was spared. He lived on. There was some good in this, and he dug deep to find it. "If I was to be bitter for twenty-two years, I wouldn't be as healthy as I am now. That could only put poison in your system and your mind."

He was around, and he was there to give back to his family and others. Today he leads a foundation that mentors inner-city youth in Chicago.

"Positive things have resulted from this, but the most positive thing I can think of right now is my son Derek and the way he has arrived with the opportunity to be an NFL football player."

And arrived he has. Derek, now twenty-eight, made it on his own. He did not play college football but took off on a career in baseball. He played in the Philadelphia Phillies organization for three seasons and saw nothing but a dead end ahead. "I didn't see my career going anywhere. I knew I wanted to try something different," he says.

Despite his lack of experience, Derek earned a spot on the roster of the Albany Firebirds of the Arena Football League. His talent served him well. In 1998 he was a candidate for Defensive Player of the Year. Hard work paid off. Derek showed good stuff to coach Bill Parcells in a tryout session, and the New York Jets signed him to their practice squad in 1999. His stint with the Jets didn't last long, but Derek continues an impressive career with the Firebirds.

We read about courage. We can only imagine the anger and bitterness Darryl had to overcome to watch his own son on the battlefield that ended his career and put him in a wheelchair for life. He faced that test in 1999 when Derek was injured in an arena game.

"I got a phone call from one of Derek's teammates. He told me he'd been injured but they didn't know to what extent. I was just stunned. I didn't know what to think. I was just hoping that lightning hadn't struck twice," Darryl says.

It turned out to be a minor concussion.

Fear disappears in the face of courage. Darryl and Derek both know that. Still, when he encouraged Derek to pursue football, Darryl spoke words few of us in his situation might have uttered: "You go out and play. Don't think about me. Just play the game like it's supposed to be played. That's what I tried to do."

That's advice any father could give. I just think it means more coming from Darryl Stingley.

SECTION 4

Pride and Prejudice

15

Notah Begay III

Just drop me off here, Dad. It's okay. I can walk."

Notah Begay pleaded with his father every morning as they neared the prestigious, private Albuquerque Academy in New Mexico.

Notah was the only Native American in the sixth grade at this fine school, and certainly the only one being driven there in an old Chevy truck that the family referred to as "Old Blue." He couldn't help but feel as out of place as that worn truck amid the BMWs and Mercedes-Benzes, couldn't hide that bite of shame when Old Blue let out its familiar backfire.

So he begged to be dropped a few blocks from the school, away from the stares of his classmates and the obvious influence of affluence.

His father wouldn't hear of it.

"No," he'd say, driving right into the parking lot amid the shiny and expensive foreign cars. "This is us."

Notah's mother, Laura Ansera-Roybal, who serves as the juvenile justice coordinator for Native Americans for the state of New Mexico, and his father, Notah II, who is a specialist for the Indian Health Service, found scholarships and took out loans so Notah could attend the academy.

Companions in Courage

They worked hard to balance the elite environment of the school with their values and social conscience. The discomfort Notah felt when he stepped from the truck, his father knew, wouldn't be fatal. But not being true to who you are? Nothing could be more dangerous. The lesson stuck with Notah as he wrestled with the contrasts of his two worlds.

Growing up in a small adobe house on the Isleta Pueblo Reservation outside of Albuquerque left him a little short of creature comforts. "For a while we had to boil hot water on a stove to take a bath," he says. In contrast, at the academy he lived amid materialism and plenty.

His athletic abilities helped buy him acceptance. He learned that being able to run, jump, and shoot could, in many people's eyes, excuse a backfiring pickup. From the sixth grade to graduation he excelled in sports and lettered in basketball, soccer, and golf.

Notah's golf beginnings were as basic and simple as his lifestyle. He was six years old when he and his brother, Clint, walked with his dad in the Twilight League at Ladera Golf Club in Albuquerque. The bug bit him big time.

"At age six I fell in love with golf," he says. "I would save money to buy practice balls. But soon my urge to practice exceeded my piggy bank. One evening I waited in the parking lot at the local public course to talk to the pro."

Begay bartered hard work in exchange for access to the course after work. His basketball coach, Mike Brown, remembers, "Notah would get out of school around 3 P.M. and practice his chipping before the gym opened at 4:40 for basketball."

As an eighth-grader, Notah was in his first state tournament in Roswell. Undaunted by the country-club atmosphere, and true to his culture, Notah drew red lines under his eyes with red clay, an Indian symbol of preparing for a challenge. He opened his corn pollen bundle and asked for blessings. His coach, Bob Verardo, remembers the other players yelling, "Woo-woo-woo! Hey, Chief, what's with the war paint?" He also remembers, "They stopped as soon as he hit the ball."

As his skills improved, Notah grew from a young kid carrying his clubs around on a bus and playing municipal courses to a mature young man with a huge golf dream. He even knew the obstacles. "I got the message," he says. "Indians aren't supposed to do this. Indians aren't supposed to do that. You can't be lawyers. You can't be doctors. And God forbid you'd be a professional golfer." He adds, "I didn't listen to it because I had this connection to the game of golf. Golf kind of grabbed me by the hand and said, 'This is going to be something that's going to do a lot of things for you.'"

At seventeen he was the top-ranked junior in the nation. As history would have it, another young phenom was breaking his own barriers. Number 2 was Tiger Woods. They were soon to be teammates at Stanford, where Notah earned a golf scholarship.

Once again, Notah's choice of school and major reflected his desire to be a role model for others. He knew that American Indians are the poorest minority in the United States and have the lowest rates of college attendance. He also knew that he already had the attention of young kids.

"I saw that I had a positive influence on them, and they kind of listened to what I had to say just based on what little amount of success I had had in golf," he says. "I realized then that I needed to get my college degree. I felt it would be hypocritical of me to give talks to Indian kids about the need for an education, staying in school and getting good grades, if I myself didn't do it. I chose a difficult school so I could go back and tell them, 'If I can do it, you can do it.'"

He graduated with a degree in economics and a list of

accomplishments that not only exemplified his commitment to excellence but underscored what he told kids: "Work harder to prove wrong those who have stereotypes and low expectations."

He was a member of Stanford's 1994 NCAA Championship team, a three-time All-America selection, holder of fifteen major junior and amateur titles. That 1994 Stanford team is a story in itself, breaking culture barriers all over the place: Tiger Woods, Will Yanagisawa, Casey Martin, Steve Burdick, and Begay.

Notah Begay III is the first full-blooded Native American to play and win on the Professional Golfers' Association Tour. "My life has changed, but I have not," he says. "This is who I am. I am an Indian."

He may have stopped coloring his cheeks but he still draws on the Keresan culture of San Felipe Pueblo. "There is great power there," he says. "I reach into my spirit and my soul and the teachings that my mom imparted onto me—believe in yourself, allow your spirit to fly free, and trust yourself."

Now he is able to fulfill his dream to be a role model for young American Indians. The week of the Kemper Open at the Tournament Players Club at Avenel, fifteen miles from Washington, D.C., Notah went to Capitol Hill to testify before the Senate Committee on Indian Affairs. His words contributed to increasing awareness of the high rates of unemployment, alcoholism, disease, suicide, and school dropouts that prevail on the reservations. He spoke eloquently to the leaders of our country, and he spoke personally to the young people his life now touches.

"I came from playing in vacant fields and overcoming odds," he says. "I'm here to tell you, I'm no different from you. I see your faces, and I see part of me in you. You all have the potential to go out and pursue what you want to do."

He makes no claims of perfection, however. He is human and can stumble—as he did in January 2000, when he was arrested and convicted on a charge of drunk driving. Did he make excuses, whine about circumstances, and try to dodge the law? No. In fact, he informed the judge about a prior out-of-state offense, guaranteeing himself a seven-day jail sentence.

"You do something wrong, you pay the price," he says.

Begay himself has more to do on the positive side of the ledger. His first name, translated from the Navajo, means "almost there." He likes to add, "But not quite."

16

Willie O'Ree

When I think of Harlem, hockey isn't what usually pops into my mind. Race surely does.

I question the origins of bigotry. I wonder why the color of a person's skin matters so much. I struggle with hatred. I admire those in the front lines of the war against it.

At P.S. 113 in Harlem, Willie O'Ree stood in front of seventy-five neighborhood kids in the cafeteria, teaching them the fundamentals of skating, hockey, and life. A new program, Ice Hockey In Harlem, invited Willie to come to inspire young African-American kids to consider hockey as their sport. Why Willie O'Ree?

Willie was the first African-American to lace up his skates in the National Hockey League. He is to hockey what Jackie Robinson is to baseball—a pioneer, one who changed the landscape and smashed the barriers holding others back.

Willie was the youngest of twelve children, so holding his own in a crowded house was good training for learning to survive on an ice surface crowded with racial taunts and high sticks. Willie first put on skates when he was three, a typical Canadian kid who loved to skate to school. As he got older, he hung out with his older brother and his friends, who played in an instructional league in Fredricton, New Brunswick.

Willie distinguished himself at every level of competition. However, playing hockey in Canada, where racism is somewhat muted, didn't prepare Willie for what he had to face when he broke into the professional ranks with the American Hockey League. The night he took the ice against Tidewater, reality cross-checked him when a black cat and cotton balls greeted him during his first shift. He played through the taunts and the disdain, through cold and malicious stares.

When Willie was called up to the Boston Bruins in 1960, he was ecstatic. The Bruins organization and his new teammates welcomed him warmly. He was greeted differently by opposing teams, as you can imagine. In a game between the Bruins and the Chicago Blackhawks the racial tension peaked. One Blackhawk butt-ended O'Ree, first with vicious racial taunts and later with the end of his stick, knocking out his front teeth. Willie responded instinctively, breaking his stick over his assailant's head. A brawl broke out when both benches emptied.

After order was restored, Willie needed a police escort to leave Chicago Stadium.

"Racist remarks from fans were much worse in the U.S. cities than in Toronto and Montreal. I particularly remember a few incidents in Chicago. The fans would yell, 'Go back to the South' and 'How come you're not picking cotton?' Things like that. It didn't bother me. Hell, I'd been called names most of my life. I just wanted to be a hockey player, and if they couldn't accept that fact, that was their problem, not mine."

Willie O'Ree completed that season, but it was his last full one in the NHL. An earlier injury, which had blinded him in his right eye, as well as the wear and tear of professional hockey, had ground down his skills. "I could deal with the racism," he said, "but not the blindness."

Even minus an eye, Willie played minor-league hockey with the San Diego Hawks in the Pacific Coast League until the 1979–80 season.

Now in his early sixties, Willie works as a security manager at a San Diego hotel and travels the country as director of the NHL's Diversity Task Force. He introduces minority children to hockey and to what it takes to overcome whatever obstacles may block their personal path.

When Willie O'Ree was honored at the 1998 All-Star Game in Vancouver, British Columbia, he was not saluted for his statistics (four goals and ten assists in forty-five NHL games) but for his courage, for standing up to racial bigotry, and for opening the door for minorities in the NHL.

Sometimes it's not about scoring goals. It's about setting and achieving them.

17

Esteban Toledo

Esteban Toledo, known as the "Grinder King" on the PGA Tour, grew up playing in a foursome with poverty, heartache, and prejudice as his associates. This is a man acquainted with adversity, who knows what it takes to persevere and succeed.

Unlike many of his fellow golfers, he didn't come of age in the plush confines of a country club. Toledo, the youngest of eleven brothers and sisters, grew up in Mexico. He began his climb to the Tour in a dirt-floor farmhouse that didn't have electricity or running water. Before Esteban was in first grade he knew how to tend livestock, pick cotton, and deal with heartbreak.

One afternoon the incessant barking of a dog got his attention. As any curious kid would, he went to see what the commotion was all about. He found the body of his murdered brother.

It's fair to say that the one tragedy spawned another. For shortly after his brother's death, Esteban's father died of a heart attack. Esteban and his mother, who never recovered from her grief, were left to tend the farm. Esteban, who did not celebrate holidays such as his birthday or Christmas, shouldered the heavy responsibility of caring for his mother and the farm at the ripe old age of eight.

In order to make more money to support his mother and the farm, Esteban began swimming across the river that separated his family farm from the Mexicali Country Club to scavenge for lost balls and sell them back to the members. As time went by and the membership of Mexicali got used to his presence, Esteban was allowed to work in the locker room and to caddy. His interest in golf took shape on blistering afternoons when the membership waited for the heat to subside.

He would make sure no suspecting eyes were following him and then he'd go out on the course and practice hitting balls. An abandoned seven-iron that he had found and kept hidden in the woods was the only club he had. Because Esteban had learned to be alert, he also became a keen observer and picked up the basics of golf's mechanics by watching members.

On those hot afternoons, he grooved the swing that he still uses today. In the evening, when he would swim back to the farm to do the chores that waited for him, he began to dream of having a complete set of clubs and playing a full round of golf.

Eventually Esteban Toledo became the proud owner of a full set of clubs—castoffs he carried in an old bag held together with wire. The daily swim, the work as a caddie, the solitary practice on the back edge of Mexicali, the farm work, and his family's grief became the heart and soul of his work ethic. At seventeen, Esteban won his first tournament with his set of orphaned clubs.

That victory brought him joy and a face-to-face confrontation with prejudice. Brown skin was not the color of choice among the members of Mexicali Country Club. He learned quickly that when it came to representing the club, white and rich was as important as golf skill. Mexicali refused to let him identify himself with it, a requirement to defend his first championship. But by this time Esteban was not going to let the racial biases of the Mexicali membership deter him. Though after being denied the opportunity to defend his title he hadn't considered playing professional golf, a wealthy American businessman discovered him hitting balls on the Mexicali range and became his sponsor and eventually his surrogate father. At eighteen, Esteban moved to the United States.

Armed with less than ten English words, self-taught golf skills, and a determination honed in the challenges of his life, he began the long journey to the PGA Tour. The Asian Tour, mini-tours in the U.S. and abroad, the Nike Tour, and numerous Q schools from 1986 brought him to the fully exempt status that he enjoys now. Mexico has now adopted Esteban as one of its favorite sons, easing some of the hurt from the time when he couldn't defend a title because of his skin.

The fans on the Tour love Esteban—he has time for everyone. Recently when he was speaking to a group of Hispanic youth, Esteban shared his secret: "I had a dream and I worked hard to make it come true. You can do that too, if you work hard and believe in yourself. Don't let anyone tell you different. When you make it, you don't have to change. I am still the same inside."

18

Ted Nolan

Growing up in northern Ontario, Canada, shaped Ted Nolan into a man. The struggles he endured provided the foundation of a philosophy of coaching that wins on the ice and in the lives of his players. Ted Nolan personifies courage, determination, and compassion, qualities that make him special.

When I reflect on what it takes to become an elite coach in professional sports, I think of videotapes, manuals, seminars on team management, hours spent behind the bench as an assistant, and time invested in understanding the psychological makeup of the modern athlete. While these ingredients are part of Nolan's background, they are not what set him apart as a coach.

Nolan was born into the Ojibway tribe on the Garden River Indian Reservation in Sault Sainte Marie, Canada. He is the third youngest of Stan and Rose Nolan's twelve children. He grew up during a time when the Canadian government believed that it could help integrate Native North Americans into society by anglicizing them—cleansing them of their language, culture, and tribal rituals.

This government policy exacted an awful toll from Nolan's family. He can remember as a seven-year-old sitting with his uncles, listening to their horrific stories of how racial intolerance and bigotry had affected them. They drank, to cope with their grief, feelings of estrangement, and worthlessness. When they died from alcohol poisoning, Ted resolved to make a difference among his native people. To him it seemed clear that respecting people and their traditions and treating them with compassion counted more than any official government policy.

Nolan's parents instilled values that helped him deal with his anger and determination to make a difference. Be respectful. Be proud of who you are. Never quit. Don't focus on what happened. Don't blame. Work with what you've got. Be happy with what you have. Be fair. Fight for justice.

While the Nolans shared the rich traditions of the Ojibway and strong family values, they were hard pressed to put food on the table every day. Some days all they had to eat was a little Indian fried bread. The old expression, "We didn't have a pot to piss in," in some ways applied to the Nolans; except that they did have a pot that Ted and his siblings employed at night. They used the same one during the day to carry water to make an ice rink in the backyard. It would take them half a day to get enough water carried from the nearby pump, but they got the job done and loved to play hockey.

On that home-constructed pond, Ted Nolan learned to skate. The equipment was shabby but he made it work. Ted's first skates were a size six; he wore a size two shoe. Padding was the ingredient that helped everything fit. The hockey was spirited, and eventually Ted, along with his brothers, began playing competitively in a house league.

They did well, but they could never play on the same shift because they had to share gloves. The lack of equipment didn't bother them but the taunting about the color of their skin did. Because Ted's mom and dad had taught him to be fair but to stand up for himself, he became a fierce competitor and fighter—qualities that have served him well as a coach and a person.

When Ted was fifteen, his father, Stan Nolan, a lumberman and welfare administrator, died of a heart attack. As Rose and the Nolan kids pulled together, she continued to encourage Ted to pursue his dream of playing professional hockey. At sixteen, Ted went to Kenora, Ontario, an eighteen-hour drive from home, to play for the Kenora Thistles in the Manitoba Junior Hockey League. But he was torn because he didn't want to leave his family in a financial lurch and because he got homesick. He cried himself to sleep every night, hoping his coach would send him home.

Phil Stafford knew Ted was struggling and encouraged him in every way possible. There was no way he was going to send him home. In spite of the difficulties, or maybe because of them, Ted excelled. A year later the Detroit Red Wings drafted him and sent him to their minor-league affiliate in Kansas City.

He stayed one night and went back home. When he walked in the house, delighted to be back, his mother looked at him and turned her back for several seconds. Then she turned and hugged him. It was her way of disapproving of his coming home. Ted headed back to Kansas City the following day.

He would return home again in 1981, not to greet his mother but to bury her. Killed by a drunk driver, she lived on for Ted as an inspiration, a source of wisdom. He would live by her credo: Be respectful. Be proud of who you are. Never quit.

Two years after his mother's death, Nolan took the ice for the Detroit Red Wings in his first NHL game.

A back injury cut short his playing days but also sent the unsuspecting Nolan bounding toward a coaching career. He'd gone home again, planning to attend college and get a business degree. The Sault Sainte Marie Greyhounds needed coaching help, and Ted reluctantly agreed to assist the current coach. A month later the owner asked Ted to coach the team.

The Greyhounds suffered through a terrible season and the town wanted Ted fired. He didn't know if he should stay or go, but something stuck in his head—the not-uncommon fan rant that "he can't coach."

Can't? Oh, Ted could hear his parents saying, "Don't quit. Can't won't work." He threw himself into becoming a coach. He contacted the six coaches he had played for; he listened; he watched; he learned how to structure practices and how to set up a game plan. The next year the Greyhounds won the league title and Ted Nolan's coaching reputation blossomed.

He won the Memorial Cup as the Greyhounds' coach, and then in 1997 the highest honor a coach can receive: NHL Coach of the Year.

Yet his defining moment came that same year when he was caught in an unfortunate power struggle among the administrative staff of the Buffalo Sabres. Several months after Ted Nolan knew he wouldn't be back as the Sabres' coach, he and I got together. I'll never forget his words.

"Pat," he said, "hockey is what I do. It's not who I am. Yes, I'm disappointed and I hope to be able to coach in the NHL again. However, in another way the Buffalo experience has turned out to be one of the best things that has ever happened to me. It has reminded me of what is important—family is more important than the power play. Taking my sons, Brandon and Jordan, to school and being a part of their lives is very special. Sandra and I are celebrating twenty years of marriage. My family continues to teach me that compassion—for myself, for my family, and for others—is the bottom line."

SECTION 5

The Fight
of Their Lives

19

Erik Fanara

Hockey, while the passion of my youth and the career of my choice, is nonetheless a game. Life in the cancer ward of any children's hospital is not. The children's hospital is the "rink" where I met the special people who have contributed so much to my life. I was the spectator to their fight with a disease in order to win life. I shared in their face-off in the struggle to overcome what at times seemed to be unfair odds. I watched the "coaches and general managers" of medicine, professional and caring doctors and nurses, set a game plan to keep the enemy from advancing. I saw the action of the nurses' station, moving throughout the ward as a team using their own strategies: chemotherapy, medication, radiation, and personal love and support, to win the battle. As a parent, I joined those who loved and cherished their children as deeply as I did my own. I ached with them and their pain and yet I learned from their hope and courage. The challenges of the ward and the rink are similar; the lessons are the same; but the consequences of victory or defeat are quite different.

Erik Fanara was five when he got cancer. He had been in and out of the hospital numerous times to be treated and evaluated. He reminded me of a seasoned hockey veteran—his courage was a constant inspiration to me. He was articulate, observant, vibrant. And, of course, he loved hockey. After I recovered from my knee surgery and started playing again, we would go over the details of every game. While on the road, I would call him and get his feedback on the game and my performance. I looked forward to his enthusiasm and fresh perspectives.

We first met when Elsie Dawe of the hospital staff came up with a fund-raising idea. The children designed ties, and Erik's carried my autograph, and we sold them to help finance a variety of programs.

Eventually, there were occasions when Erik was able to come to a Sabres practice. He became the team's good-luck charm. All the players knew him. As our friendship grew, my admiration for Erik's perseverance increased as well. The love he and his parents shared with one another was incredible to me. They didn't focus on being victimized by the terrible disease that afflicted their family. Erik's parents were loving and supportive of anything that would be a positive and hopeful experience for the one they treasured so much and felt so helpless to heal. Erik continued to be an integral part of my life.

Little did I know that my journey to give back would result in being given so much. I was so touched by his life and attitude that when I was awarded the Masterton Trophy, I spoke to Erik over the television. I dedicated the award to him because athletes were chosen for perseverance, courage, and dedication. I told him that he embodied all three.

Erik lost his battle to cancer on January 16, 1996. While all of us who had known Erik grieved his passing, we had all been strengthened and inspired by his courageous battle. His funeral was a powerful experience. Erik would hug us all one more time before his funeral was over.

January 20 was a gray, cold day. The somber weather

matched our collective mood as we sat and listened to the music at the beginning of Erik's funeral service. After a number of people eulogized him, his mother stood and asked us to stand and hold hands in remembrance of her son. She called him her "little angel" and said the song he liked to sing to her, and for her to hear, was "You Are My Sunshine." Then she started singing, and in a moment all of us joined her in tribute to Erik. As we sang, the sun started pouring through the stained-glass window in the front of the church. Embraced by its warmth, there was not a person who wasn't crying, singing, and feeling that Erik was there with us. When I looked down at the tie that Erik had designed and then looked back toward the window, the light shined through stained-glass images of rainbows, stars, clouds, and animals. They were the same images that Erik put on the tie. The sunlit faces of Jesus and Mary gave me the sensation that Erik had gathered all of heaven together to be with us as we said good-bye to his earthly existence.

In the game of life, there are wins and losses. This relationship of strength and courage centered on a very special tie.

20

Aaron Graves

It's not how *long* a person lives that determines the quality of his life. It's *how* he lives. Since my initial experience with death, when my junior high school friend John Brown died, I have grown in my admiration for how creative and powerful people can be when facing death. They've showed me that while the human body perishes, the spirit of the person never dies. The story of Aaron Graves is proof of our eternal nature.

Aaron was a young man who lived his life full measure, even though he was just seventeen when he died on December 22, 1999. Stricken with a rare form of cancer, Aaron showed us in death how to live.

When Aaron was diagnosed, the doctor told his parents he would be their source of strength. You would think it would be the other way around, but the doctor was right. When it became apparent that Aaron wasn't going to make it, his parents tried their best to be strong and positive and to keep their devastation and grief to themselves. Who helped them with the reality that he would soon be saying good-bye? Aaron.

"He is our hero. His strength and courage enable my husband and I and Aaron's brother, Johnny, to get through this together," was what his mom, Michele, said. "It seemed like the whole world was his friend. He never complained about his pain and he was always happy."

Aaron spent three months at Memorial Sloan-Kettering Cancer Center in New York City. After that stay, he and his family made monthly trips to continue his care. Even though those treatments left him disoriented and weak, his primary concern was getting back on the basketball court with the St. Joseph's team in Buffalo.

Aaron loved and thrived on athletic competition. He started playing soccer when he was four years old, in the Delaware Soccer League. He was captain of the St. Joe's freshman soccer team. In 1998 he played guard on the St. Joe's junior varsity basketball team. The last year of Aaron's life, he would come back from his treatments in New York and head for practice with the varsity. He was so weak he could hardly get up and down the court, but his presence and determination inspired his teammates and the whole St. Joe's community.

Aaron Graves was not only an athlete, he was a scholar. He made the honor roll at the first marking period a few months before he passed away. Aaron loved art and music. He attended the Western New York Academy of Dance for ten years and became an excellent tap dancer. Before and after his treatment, Aaron painted an acrylic reproduction of Monet's *Regatta at Sainte-Addresse*. After his death Aaron's family donated his painting to St. Joe's to raise scholarship money for the school. His father, Eugene Graves, was the highest bidder, and the painting now hangs in the Graveses' living room.

In addition to athletics, academics, and his extracurricular activities, Aaron made his mark in his community. When he wasn't delivering the *Buffalo News* to his neighborhood, he volunteered with the Buffalo Police Department, where his mom works, the Kiwanis Club, and the

Parkside Community Association, or counseled kids at the Parkside Summer Arts Program. He did his counseling despite a broken arm, the result of bones made brittle by his cancer treatment.

Even though Aaron was fighting for his own life, he never stopped reaching out to help those around him. "He was a courageous young man who never complained and was always polite and respectful. He was one of a kind. He had a drive for life," says Police Commissioner Rocco Diina.

Aaron died as he lived—giving life and energy to those around him. Eighteen hundred people attended Aaron's funeral to celebrate his life. The police department in parade dress, the singers from St. Joseph Collegiate Institute, his church, and his family and friends said good-bye to a young man whose influence touched the lives of many people.

His family still mourns his loss. The Buffalo community and the student body of St. Joe's miss his energy and upbeat take on life and death. Yet they feel his presence, they see his smile, they hear his words, and they remember his attitude. An anonymous scholarship has been established at St. Joe's in Aaron's honor.

The two stipulations: academic achievement and community service. That's Aaron's legacy. It connects us with him and his memory, and those thoughts and feelings will never die.

21

Kathy Waldo

Kathy Waldo might have spent her days staring at the walls and wondering what an active life is all about.

But no walls hemmed her in. If she observed any boundaries, respected any barriers, they were the ones a hockey rink provides naturally. Kathy Waldo crashed into the boards many a time but never hit the wall.

She was the first girl to play on her high school's boys' hockey team and the first to be named captain. She went on to star at Northeastern University. She's one of my Companions in Courage, but her ever-present companion was, and is, cystic fibrosis.

Two months after she was born in Cross Plains, Wisconsin, some twenty years ago, her parents, Joe and Maureen Waldo, brought their little girl to the doctor's office because of lingering congestion in her chest. Neither the diagnosis nor the prognosis raised anyone's spirits.

"Kathy would have to spend her life in and out of hospitals," her mother remembers the doctors saying. "They told us our daughter would live until she was eighteen, maybe twenty, and that would be that."

The symptoms were ugly. People with CF suffer from chronic lung infections and digestive disorders. A sticky, thick mucus, which is difficult to remove and promotes bacterial infection, eats away at the lung tissue. Excessive appetite along with poor weight gain often adds to the frailty of an already vulnerable immune system. The coughing spells, frightening infections, and just plain exhaustion often lead to frequent hospitalizations and continuous use of antibiotics, enzyme supplements, and other medications.

Joe and Maureen spent many nights considering possible courses of action. They elected to take a risk and be different. "We decided to take our own approach. She was not going to grow up as a patient," Maureen says. "She deserved more."

They figured a sedentary existence in a hospital room wouldn't help the breathing. They believed that running and playing and literally gulping in the fresh air would be so much more natural and healing. So whenever one of those deep, racking spells of coughing hit, Joe would make Kathy go out and run around the block. They encouraged David, her older brother, to include Kathy in football, baseball, and basketball.

Maybe, just maybe, there was something in the air. At three years of age, Kathy followed David onto the ice to play hockey. Picture this little tyke strapping on skates and joining a boys' Midget team for four- to seven-year-olds. Guess what? She was great. And so was this self-developed therapy.

"Nothing's better for me than hockey," Kathy says. "The skating makes you work really hard, and then you take in the cold air from the ice. It opens your lungs up and keeps things moving in your body."

Remember those warnings of a short life marred by hospital stays? Kathy was only hospitalized twice by the time she was eighteen.

Maybe it sounds easy because it worked so well. But I call Kathy a Companion in Courage because all of this was so much harder and more treacherous than it seems. Every time she coughs or gets a cold, or is even near someone with a cold, a warning light flashes in her mind. She must be scrupulous in safeguarding her precious health. She must maintain her regimen of medication to continually break down the mucus buildup in her lungs. Infection still comes all too easily.

After her freshman year at Northeastern, surgery to repair a shoulder injury went well, but complications—a lung infection—followed. She had to fight off more severe consequences with intravenous fluids and constant trips back and forth from the hospital.

"It reminds me of what can happen," says Kathy. "It was horrible."

And yet it also puts her in mind of how awful a quiet, inactive existence would be. Her motto is simple: Be tough. She has a life. She's going to live it.

"People who sit around and complain about life—that sucks," Kathy says. "I know I have a disease that's technically supposed to give me a shorter life span. But why should I think about dying? I've beaten the odds, and I'll continue to beat the odds."

That's why Kathy Waldo is not only a Companion in Courage but a breath of fresh air.

22

John Cullen

John Cullen absorbed many hits as a star center for the Pittsburgh Penguins and the Tampa Bay Lightning, but none flattened him like the news he received in the spring of 1997.

He went to the doctor to check out his flulike symptoms and the X-ray/CT scan showed a baseball-size tumor in his chest. He had non-Hodgkin's lymphoma. But he was a picture of perfect health and superb conditioning. Non-Hodgkin's lymphoma? Impossible!

John recovered from the shock of the medical findings and began a rigorous regimen of chemotherapy and exercise. "He lost his hair and had pain from the chemo, but he worked right through it," said John McCortney, his personal trainer. "He ran, lifted, everything. He got stronger."

The tumor disappeared in September 1997, but John's body still housed cancer cells and doctors told him he had a fifty-fifty chance of survival. His season was finished without ever beginning, but his number 12 took the ice in every game, worn on the uniform sleeves of his teammates in tribute to their valiant colleague.

While his teammates battled on the ice, Cullen fought for his life off it. John began another round of chemotherapy and radiation. He had his weights and a stationary bike brought to his room. Even though he was too weak to use them, they provided incentive and gave him the motivation to fight this terrible disease.

In early October a nurse and Cullen's wife, Valerie, were wheeling him to a radiation treatment when, suddenly and without warning, he slumped in his chair. The nurse checked his pulse and found nothing. His heart had stopped beating. Doctors heard her screaming, "Code Blue! Code Blue!" and rushed to revive John with a defibrillator.

Sure, it sounds like one of those television shows. But if there was going to be a happy ending, no one could imagine it. Not long after cheating death, John needed a bone marrow transplant. His marrow had to be harvested, cleansed, and reintroduced. Even though on the second day of the procedure he developed pericarditis, an inflammation of the sac surrounding the heart, John battled the odds and won.

When John and Valerie returned to Tampa that winter, he was a shell of his former self, frail and weak. He had trouble keeping up with Valerie and his daughter, Kennedy, when they took short walks together. But John began to get his strength back. In April he returned to Boston for a checkup and received good news—the cancer was no longer living in his body. He came back to Tampa with one objective: to play hockey for the Tampa Bay Lightning.

When he began training camp that next autumn, John didn't know what to expect. He started camp tentatively, giving himself time to get his legs back and let his body adjust to a different kind of battle—hockey in the NHL. He knew he had recovered his touch when he scored the winning goal in the last exhibition game of the season. It came against the best goalie in the league, Dominik Hasek of the Buffalo Sabres.

On October 6, 1998, John Cullen took the opening face-off in the Lightning's first game of the season.

"Exciting days! But you don't go through a cancer ordeal, with all the treatment, without changing. I've changed spiritually, physically, and emotionally. I don't want sympathy. It will weaken me," John said.

Well, how about a little admiration? No professional athlete had returned to play after undergoing a bone marrow transplant.

Cullen didn't play much in the next three Tampa games and then sat the next four. His coach, Jacques Demers, whose wife was battling cancer, approached John about taking an assistant coaching position with the team. John, who was not satisfied with his comeback progress, thanked Jacques for the offer but decided instead to play for Tampa's IHL team, the Cleveland Lumberjacks.

He got off to a quick start, but he also came down with the flu and bronchitis, and a nagging fear arose that his body could not endure this rigorous game anymore. John had to face the reality that the bone-rattling checks of professional hockey were too much for him. He returned home to discuss his future with his wife and their friends.

On November 27 John Cullen retired and accepted the job as assistant coach of the Tampa Bay Lightning. The last twenty months of his life had scaled the heights and plumbed the depths and left him with a lesson learned.

"Anytime a person plays a game as long as I have it is difficult to say good-bye. I know I have made the right decision," he said. "It is time to be realistic and move on to a new challenge. My goal was to make it back, and I achieved that. I am grateful to the many people who supported and encouraged me. I went through a lot. I went through extensive cancer treatment and survived. Now I want to get my story out to give hope to people who are battling cancer."

He set too modest a goal. He gives hope to us all.

23

Jimmie Heuga

One in a thousand people is stricken with multiple sclerosis. Sometimes that person turns out to be one in a million.

In 1970, Jimmie Heuga, one of the first American men to be awarded an Olympic Alpine skiing medal, was diagnosed with this progressive, crippling disease of the immune system, in which the mylan sheath that covers nerve endings becomes scarred and the brain's instructions can no longer get to parts of the body.

Just as the disease slowly takes away bits of your life, so will the people sworn to protect you. Not out of meanness, but out of love and caring. So the doctors ordered the bronze medalist in the 1964 Innsbruck Winter Games to refrain from any athletic activity. The sport in which he excelled had become too dangerous, and his body couldn't handle the stress of training.

How in the world does a great athlete take a blow like that?

I have been on injured reserve for periods of time and can hardly describe the frustration of not competing. I know I couldn't wait to return to the ice and I probably drove everybody around me crazy until I could.

Well, Jimmie got the message that he would never compete on the slopes again. Soon the crippling effects of the degenerative disease began to affect his daily life. His vision would blur and feeling from the waist down would numb. He was supposed to avoid stress. So easy to say. His marriage began to fail, his hero role vanished, and he headed slowly downhill, as if the race was over. By 1975 he had given up and lived as a recluse, frustrated and depressed.

You'll read the story later of another of my Companions in Courage, Zoe Koplowitz, whose moment of clarity came from a vitamin pill that she could not swallow. Well, Jimmie's arrived as he sat by himself, a book in his hand. In his reading he was drawn to a quote by the philosopher Blaise Pascal.

" 'One of man's greatest obstacles is to learn to sit quietly in his room,' " Jimmie recalls. "What that quote said to me was, 'This is the rest of your life. You can sit here and feel sorry for yourself, or you can get back into life.' "

Jimmie drew this from it: "I just couldn't stand around waiting for a magical cure."

To move forward, Jimmie looked to his past. He rekindled the same spirit in which he had trained for skiing in his youth in Squaw Valley, California. He developed his own cardiovascular workout. This included push-ups, sit-ups, swimming, and bike riding. He slowly got his positive spirit back. In fact he retrieved life itself. Like Zoe, he found more meaning in life by giving to those who suffer.

In 1984 Jimmie founded the Jimmie Heuga Center for the Reanimation of the Physically Challenged, in Edwards, Colorado. There he developed a revolutionary approach to living with MS, with a focus on physical activity. "I'm the least qualified person to run a medical center," says Jimmie, "but I do know how to live. You can't just wait for the lights to be shut off."

He did not do all of this by himself. I am once again moved by the companions in Jimmie's life who gave their love and support and in turn received such a large reward.

First came romance, with marketing executive Debbie Dana. She was engaged when they met, so he was very cautious about asking her out. She had just been through brain surgery herself and told Jimmie that she felt newly alive and in touch with the world. So Jimmie made his move. "In our next life, I'd like to get together with you," he said. Debbie responded, "I think this is my next life."

Love's magic did the rest. Debbie's years of caring for Jimmie, who now uses a wheelchair, epitomize the true spirit of loving. Jimmie is all but helpless. After all these years Debbie has concluded, "In physique, Jimmie is very small. Yet he has so much heart he is the biggest man I know."

A second inspiration in Jimmie's life was his lasting friendship with Billy Kidd, the companion in the 1964 Olympics who came in a whisker ahead of Jimmie for the silver medal. For over thirty years their friendship has deepened. Kidd is on the board of the Jimmie Heuga Center and is godfather to two of Jimmie's sons. Jimmie in turn is godfather to Kidd's daughter, Hayley. Their friendship has been an irreplaceable source of encouragement to Jimmie.

"Jimmie is an inspiration to everyone," Kidd says. "He doesn't think about MS as a disability, but as a challenge."

And he never could have imagined that he'd win his uphill battles the same way he won the downhill.

24

Annie Leight

Annie Leight had a vision. A vision and a goal. To usher in the new millennium as a time of transition and transformation, she planned to walk 10,000 miles on a route shaped like a butterfly.

Why a butterfly? To symbolize new times, freedom, personal evolution, in the same way a caterpillar disappears into a cocoon and emerges ready to fly.

Talk about a huge aspiration. To walk 10,000 miles? And Annie would accomplish her mission—at least in part. She would ultimately complete 3,300 miles of her visionary project, slowed at first by injuries suffered in a car accident, and stopped finally by cancer.

She had planned to begin in October of 1993, but spent two years recovering and rehabilitating after the accident. And even as she healed, doctors hit her with the cancer diagnosis.

Annie and her husband, Rob, grieved, but Annie's walk kept growing in importance. And they decided to make the walk the focal point of her battle against her disease. "Most people assume that when you're diagnosed with cancer, you're going to follow a tried-and-true path. What my husband and friends did was give me permission to go on my own journey and to live out my own vision," Annie said. "My walk had become a sacred task, the outcome of which I did not know. I could do nothing else. In spite of the setbacks, it was my mission."

Neither her injuries nor cancer would keep her from her goal. She would walk hampered by the effects of both, but she would walk nonetheless.

"What I consciously wanted to do was to open my heart and, at least on a small scale, mirror other ways of being alive," she said. "Everybody should have dignity and respect. Because if we don't, we don't have anything."

Wow. What a clarity of purpose and sense of meaning.

Annie began her walk on January 1, 1997. And she continued for eight months, before the ravages of cancer forced her from the road.

Rick Murrie Stearns, publisher of *Personal Transformations* magazine, interviewed Annie a week before she died. She was bedridden in a motel not far from where her walk had ended, and she was celebrating every step she had taken.

"The walk brought me into a relationship with everything at very, very deep levels," she told Stearns. "Physically, at first, the walk was agony because of all the pain. So the first six months was a conscious commitment, sometimes for five minutes, just to stay with the walk."

So how did she cope and continue driving herself?

"I learned that all we have is now. I also learned that even though I was fifty years old, I could be remarkably resilient. One of the main things I learned was how to stay with something. Being and living in nature much of the time, I learned that there is a softness underlying all of life—a gentleness, a tenderness. Learning to trust that became very important for coping. I could simply be present to anything. The walk allowed me not only to have a connecting point but to have a place where there's no disconnect. I learned that to be open to life, instead of fending life off, allows for each moment to count. I want to say to everyone: Live your life in the present moment."

Didn't she fear dying?

"I'm not afraid anymore," she told Stearns. "I could get back into fear in the next five minutes. I assume fear is always a companion. It is a matter of what kind of allegiance it's given and how much energy is devoted to it. It's like breath is there, or like the capacity for joy and love and awe is there. You just don't have to feed it. I feel that I am in a relationship with God now; like I am one with God. That is real stuff for me, not just conceptual like it used to be. It is no longer a concept. Right now it's my way of being alive in the world."

At the end of their conversation, Stearns asked Annie what thoughts she wanted us to take away from her journey.

"Stay with your own life," she said. "Don't get distracted by trying to be somebody else. Learn to enjoy and be open to the beauty of any moment, even though there may be enormous pain, ugliness, and injustice. Finally, risk opening your heart to love and allow the beauty of love into your life as much of the time as possible."

Butterflies vanish with the season, their beauty a memory. Love never ends. Love never fails.

25

Travis Roy

Meet Travis Roy, college graduate. Five years after enrolling at Boston University, there he was, getting his degree in communications in May of 2000. Sadly, Travis could not walk over to the dean, accept his diploma, and enjoy a hearty handshake. There's more to his story than academic pursuits and the minting of another graduate.

Travis Roy went to BU to play ice hockey. That's where his future lay. That would be his career path. But his college hockey career lasted eleven seconds. It had barely begun, yet it—and life as Travis and his family knew it—had ended.

Travis, a freshman, took his first shift on October 20, 1995, and eleven ticks of the clock later slammed headfirst into the boards. He tried to get up but he couldn't move. The ominous silence that filled the hockey arena made the tragic scene unfolding on the ice even more scary. The Roy family credo—"Get up. You're not hurt"—echoed in Travis's head, but he could not comply. The connection between his thoughts and his body was broken.

What a sad and horrible fate for anyone. But think for a moment about athletes and the special relationship they have with their bodies. They hone their reflexes, develop wonderful specialized skills, and live fast-paced, action-oriented lives. And in an accident such as Travis's, suddenly all of it—not only what they worked for but what their core being strove for—no longer exists.

Christopher Reeve, a fine actor and equestrian, suffered a spinal cord injury in a fall from a horse. You know how he has labored to direct films from his wheelchair, the war he fights just to survive each day. You've heard how hard he has worked to raise funds for research into finding a cure for paralysis. Much the same can be said for Marc Buoniconti, a college football player (and son of famous Miami Dolphins linebacker Nick Buoniconti) injured and rendered quadriplegic in a game. And there's a wonderful story to be told about Tim Strachan, a promising high school quarterback who suffered a horrible neck injury in a swimming accident before he went off to the University of Maryland. Strachan, in a wheelchair, certainly couldn't play for Maryland, but the school gave him his scholarship nonetheless and he found a new outlet in working the sidelines for the radio station that broadcasts the Terrapins' games.

Now Travis's father, a former Division I MVP at the University of Vermont, knew Travis was in trouble within seconds of that head-on collision. Lee had never seen his son lie on the ice without moving. Brenda and Dodi, Travis's mother and sister, along with Tim Pratt, Travis's last high school coach, watched nervously while Lee bent over his son. Travis did not move.

When Dodi, a nurse, got to her brother, she knew he was in trouble. Her father was crying. Travis's first words when his father reached his side were, "Dad, I'm in deep s——. My neck hurts and I can't feel my arms or legs. But, Dad, I made it." Lee responded, "You're right, son. You made it to Division I hockey."

Travis's coach at BU, Jack Parker, walked to where his

player was lying on the ice. His heart sank when he saw Travis talking. Hockey players move their legs first to reassure themselves that they are going to be able to keep skating. Parker had never seen a player down on the ice who didn't move his legs and talk at the same time. Travis was placed carefully on a stretcher and taken to Boston City Hospital. X-rays confirmed the Roys' worst fears—quadriplegia, with a slim chance of recovery.

Travis's fourth cervical vertebra was seriously damaged. It had exploded when his head hit the boards. Travis's brain could no longer send signals to the rest of his body.

He underwent surgery to stabilize his neck and remove the bone fragments lodged in his spine and back. He came down with pneumonia and developed stomach ulcers from the steroids that were being pumped into his system. His temperature went off the charts and his right lung collapsed. For two weeks he was fed through one tube while he received air through another tube. When the tubes were removed, Travis had to have a tracheotomy in order to breathe. This made it impossible for him to talk. His ability to communicate was reduced to eye blinks, slight nods, and occasional smiles. When asked if he were angry, he shook his head, "No." Asked if he was sad, he nodded, "Yes."

Not much has changed for Travis's body in the time since the injury. He is still listed as a quadriplegic with a poor prognosis; however, the indomitable spirit that motivated him to become a Division I hockey player is still very much alive and well. How does a talented, hardworking athlete move on after such a tragedy? A review of what brought Travis to that Boston University rink that fateful October day answers that question.

When Travis was born in April 1975, his father was the manager of the Kennebec Ice Arena. Shortly after his birth the family moved to Yarmouth, Maine, where Lee managed the North Yarmouth Academy rink. One might say that Travis was born to be on the ice. He was twenty months old when he shuffled across the Yarmouth ice in a pair of figure skates. By age three he was skating with kids ages four to eight because his father didn't have enough players to field a pre-mite team.

Hockey in Maine was not a sport that attracted many kids during the seventies. Over the next four years Lee alternated Travis between offense and defense, so he would learn all aspects of the game. When Lee accepted the assistant director's job at the Cumberland Civic Center, the home of the Philadelphia Flyers' minor-league team, the Maine Mariners, Travis would accompany his dad to watch the Mariners practice. At an early age he became a student of the game. When he turned seven, Mariners general manager and coach Tom McVie made Travis the team stickboy and locker-room gofer. He kept water bottles full, carried tape, supplied gum—he was always bringing the players something. It wasn't long before Travis was an integral part of the Mariners team.

For nine years Travis was in the Mariners locker room, soaking up every bit of hockey knowledge and strategy he could from the likes of John Paddock, Mike Milbury, Rick Bowness, and E. J. McGuire. He skated with some of the players after practice and occasionally went on road trips with the team. By the time he reached high school, he had a knowledge of hockey rare in a teenager and a savvy that offset his average speed and lack of size.

Travis played at Yarmouth High and moved over to Yarmouth Academy, where he made all-state as a forward. In order to get more exposure and play against tougher competition, Travis transferred to a Massachusetts prep school, Tabor, for his junior and senior years, where he distinguished himself. At age eighteen he made the prestigious Hockey Night in Boston summer league. He was one of six players selected from the summer tournament as most likely to make it in the pros.

Academically, Travis had to work hard to maintain his grades, but he brought the same determination to his studies that he displayed on the ice. In the words of one of his teachers, "Travis was an overachiever."

The summer before college started, Travis worked in Boston and lifted weights to get ready for the season. When practice began, Travis was thrilled to be on the ice of a Division I champion. Midnight Madness opened the season for BU. "We Are the Champions" blasted from the PA system. Travis felt overwhelmed with emotion and pride. He was achieving the goals he had set for himself back when he was fourteen. Jack Parker and Travis's BU teammates were impressed with his hockey skills and how knowledgeable he was in all three ice zones. It came as no surprise that he made the team.

Two days before the first game, against North Dakota, Parker told him that he would be playing the first shift of the game, and, in the second game, against Vermont, his dad's college team, he would be skating on the first line. The Roys and Travis were ecstatic at the news—dreams were becoming reality.

Eleven seconds into his first shift all of that changed. Travis was primed to distinguish himself in Division I and professional hockey. All the preparation, the ability to focus, to take nothing for granted, to see all three zones—the big picture—would no longer be needed on the ice. Travis was in a contest for his life.

"I still prepare each day just as I did when I could skate. My equipment is no longer pads and skates, it's medicine and medical apparatus. My body is lifeless but my mind is alive," he says. "Do I have regrets? Yes! Am I grateful? Yes! Do I get discouraged? Yes! Do I still have goals? Yes! I take nothing for granted but I live each day thankful that I can still push breath through my lungs. I no longer dodge checks and put pucks in nets. I elude the temptation to dwell on the past and feel sorry for myself. Each day I am determined to use my mind, my attitude, and the ability I have to the fullest of my capacity. I approach life the same way I approached hockey: I give it my best."

26

Simon Keith

We always talk about the heart of a champion. And that's one part of Simon Keith's amazing story. Amazing because the heart of this champion came from someone else. Yes. Simon Keith, professional soccer player, is also Simon Keith, transplant survivor.

I relate deeply to his ordeal because I can identify with his childhood passion and what he went through to achieve his goal. Though I was born in America, my early departure from home to play junior hockey in Montreal deepened my awareness of what hockey meant to every young athlete in Canada. Well, imagine the focus on soccer for young Simon, growing up in Lewes, England, with a father who had played semipro soccer in the fifties. It was so much a part of their lives as a family.

Even after they moved to Vancouver, British Columbia, their passion never diminished. Simon's father, David, was an assistant coach for the Canadian team in 1982, and Simon started playing when he was four. He was always an outstanding performer. After high school, his exceptional talent landed him a spot on the roster of Millwall, then a third-division team in England.

Good things kept coming. As word of Simon's talent got

around, he was given one of the sixteen spots on the Canadian development team. The team trained in Victoria so Simon stayed at home and enrolled at the University of Victoria in the fall of 1984. He played with passion and dedication, working hard to continue to improve his skills and his love for the game. His heart was in his feet.

As with any well-conditioned athlete, the first signs of physical trouble are often met with a casual diagnosis. It's in your head! You're under too much stress! It's an attitude problem. Maybe you just need a rest.

But Simon knew something was wrong. He tired too easily. He was more vulnerable to the elements than he had ever been before.

"One day at practice," he says, "I was freezing, so I had my hands in my pockets. My coach yelled at me to take them out. When I did, they were pure white. A few minutes later the coach chewed me out again for having my hands in my pockets. I didn't even know I had put them back in there."

The coach called Simon aside and told him he had a bad attitude. Simon and his family saw it differently. They searched for answers. They met with many frustrations, including assorted medical misdiagnoses.

A doctor at Vancouver General Hospital finally nailed it. Simon's heart had been damaged by a virus. A biopsy revealed viral myocarditis. It had destroyed part of the heart muscle and the heart could not pump blood effectively, causing poor circulation and early fatigue.

Medicine and steroids worked so well that Simon became known locally as the "miracle boy." He returned to the team and earned all-Canada honors. But once he was weaned from the steroids, his symptoms returned. It took longer to recover from a workout and fatigue grew more commonplace.

In February 1986, Simon again visited Vancouver General Hospital. Another biopsy. Another diagnosis: "Your heart is too damaged. You need a transplant or you're dead."

This was a difficult prescription to follow. Simon went first to the biggest transplant center in Canada, University Hospital in London, Ontario. He was accepted as a candidate. Oddly, they found him too healthy to take priority over others nearer death. In essence they said, "Come back when you're worse."

Referred to Dr. Terence English, a transplant surgeon at Papworth Hospital in Cambridge, England, Simon finally heard the long-awaited words about a heart transplant: "If you want one, we'll give you one."

That summer, a seventeen-year-old boy died of a brain hemorrhage while playing soccer. His heart was transplanted into Simon's body the next day. Two and a half months later Simon returned to Canada to a hero's welcome. They loved him and they loved his story. They adopted him. They protected him. "I would go out and want to have a beer, and there would be somebody there saying I shouldn't."

In the fall he began his courageous comeback to the world he loved. He enrolled at UNLV and signed up for the soccer team. The concern was overwhelming. Liability releases were signed and reassurances were given. Simon told his coach, Barry Barto, "Look, if I die, I die. But I won't. I promise you."

His courage and heart were back in his feet. Named all–Big West his junior and senior years, he was chosen student athlete of the year by the conference and in April was invited to the All-Star Game, an honor given only to the top thirty seniors in the country.

And now the incredible finale. Simon's collegiate accomplishments were brought to the attention of Cleveland Crunch general manager Al Miller, who made him the first pick in the 1989 Major Indoor Soccer League draft. Certainly there are risks, but Simon made his choice and is an inspiration to all. He says of his fans, "They're really glad I'm doing what I'm doing because it inspires somebody, somewhere along the line. Whether it's their sick aunt, brother, dad, whatever, it makes me feel good."

You could probably say it warms his heart.

27

Karen Smyers

I always marvel at the stern stuff so many of my Companions in Courage find in their hearts and in their spirits.

They cope with horrible diseases and treatments that can be nearly as bad. Yet they throw themselves no pity parties and they don't expend valuable energy carping and complaining.

That's one of the most touching things in Karen Smyers's story. She did not let any of the awful things that befell her keep her from the goal of trying to make the United States Olympic triathlon team. But she did cry once, which I think you'll find understandable, coming as it did during her battle with cancer, her recovery from a severed artery in her leg, and from massive injuries suffered when a truck hit her as she trained on her bicycle.

The tears burst forth in Ixtapa, Mexico, not long after Karen learned she had thyroid cancer. It was September of 1999 and those swollen glands in her neck were not, as she had originally believed, the result of bronchitis. She raced anyway and, in a collision with another cyclist, broke her collarbone. But that's not when she cried.

Bandaged, in pain, unable to carry her own luggage, she went to the airport to return to her home in Lincoln, Massachusetts, and pleaded for a courtesy upgrade to business class. She was turned down. And then came the torrent, forty-five minutes of sobbing.

"Once I got that out of my system, I was fine," she says.

Fine? How many of us would describe ourselves that way after living through a fraction of the injuries and ordeals she has suffered? Wow. But here's how Karen looks at life: "If I've learned anything, it's the value of flexibility and re-siliency."

Karen, a three-sport star at Wethersfield High School in Connecticut, swam at Princeton University and continued to run as an additional way to train. In 1984 in Cambridge, Massachusetts, she competed in her first short triathlon: an 800-meter swim, 8-mile bike ride, and 3-mile run. She borrowed a bike and won that race. A year later she turned pro.

In 1990 she won the world's triathlon title. By 1995 she dominated the sport, winning the world championship in Cancún, taking first at the Pan Am Games and in the Iron-man Hawaii. She had never missed a race because of an injury or failed to finish one she started. Maybe her competitors couldn't catch up with her, but fate could, and did.

In April of 1997, while cleaning her house, Karen tried to remove the storm windows. As she held one overhead, the glass broke and one large shard dropped onto the back of her leg, severing her hamstring. She dragged herself across the floor to reach the phone and call 911. Then she spent six months rehabbing the injury.

Jump ahead fourteen months. Having just given birth to her daughter, Jenna, Karen went back into training, ener-gized by motherhood and the time off from her sport. While out on her bike she got clipped by a truck and went sailing through the air. She suffered six broken ribs, a lung contusion, a separated shoulder, and a bunch of bruises.

Worse than missing her second straight Ironman Hawaii,

worse than another training setback, was the terrible feeling that she was not being all the mother she could to Jenna. She couldn't pick up her daughter or nurse her without assistance.

But she healed. A little more than a year after that truck nailed her, she finished second in Hawaii. And then came the cancer surgery in December of 1999, with doctors removing half of her thyroid. Once again she had to jumpstart her career, recover from the surgery and that injured shoulder, and claw her way back into the type of condition that the triathlon demands. She finished seventh in the Olympic trials, not good enough to qualify for the trip to Sydney, Australia.

"I just tried to get every ounce of my body that I could, all the way to the end," she says. "I think I did that and it just ended up not being quite enough."

Next came another enforced layoff, for radioactive iodine treatment for the thyroid. After that, you can be sure she'll be back in training, preparing for the next competition. "It's what she loves doing," says her husband, Bill. "And it's the way she wants to live her life."

Somewhere along the line, Karen Smyers learned that life is not a sprint. It's a marathon, maybe even a triathlon.

"People look at me now and think of me as this hardluck kid," she says. "But I take a look at my life, what I'm doing, what I have, and the life I've lived. I keep thinking, 'I'm incredibly charmed.' I've had a couple hurdles but I think, in the grand scheme of things, I'm so fortunate."

28

Tom Dolan

Tom Dolan loves to compete. He loves to swim and he loves to excel. There's only one problem—he has trouble getting air into his lungs. The combination of allergies, asthma, and competitive swimming has not made breathing easy for this world-class swimmer. These difficulties have only strengthened Tom's resolve to be the best in the world. Believe me, I know about asthma firsthand, and it only makes me respect Tom Dolan more. In the face of others wanting you to cut back or give up, you have to bear down even harder, not only to overcome the lack of air but also the sense that you "can't do it" or even worse, you "shouldn't do it."

Tom's determination and workout schedule clash head-on with his body when it protests the demands of his training regimen. Tom has a narrow windpipe that does not allow enough air into his lungs. Under normal circumstances his tight air passage, with the exception of some wheezing, might not present a problem; however, Tom's circumstances never seem to be normal.

His parents, Bill and Jef, have always held their breath while Tom was fighting to find his. Ever since he was a young boy, he would push himself to the edge of danger in whatever he did. It didn't matter what the activity or sport was, Tom approached it with a devil-may-care attitude. He went full throttle in whatever he did. While his father worries that Tom doesn't have a well-developed sense of self-preservation, he is proud of Tom's athletic accomplishments as a swimmer. His mother, recalling his ninety-mile-an-hour childhood thrill rides down hills on his Big Wheel, is grateful Tom is still alive.

Tom began his swimming career at the age of five. He wanted to do whatever his sister, Kathleen, did. She swam, so he swam. And he didn't rest until he beat her. At fifteen, Dolan won three titles at the Junior Nationals. When he was eighteen he set the world record in the 400-meter individual medley as the youngest male member of the U.S. team. During his career at the University of Michigan he set three U.S. records and was twice named the NCAA swimmer of the year. He won gold medals in the 400-meter individual medley at the 1996 and 2000 Olympics, as well as a silver medal in the 200-meter individual medley at the 2000 Olympics in Sydney.

There is no question about Tom Dolan's talent, but I am not sharing his story because of his ability. What inspires me about Tom is that he has never let his physical handicaps deter him. His determination, fueled by his courage, pushed him to succeed at what he loves.

Yes, he has passed out in the pool. Yes, he has had to use an inhaler to be able to climb out of the pool before he drowned. Yes, he has had to grab lane ropes at times to keep from going under. Yes, he has scared his parents and his coach, Joe Urbanchek. Yes, he developed chronic fatigue from his demanding work schedule.

And yet he lives a full and varied life. When Tom is not swimming, he is playing in his rap band, MC (Mass Confusion), or hanging out with his friends. His zest for just being alive every day reflects itself in all he does. After the

1996 Olympics, Dolan was interviewed by Broderick Turner, a thirteen-year-old. Broderick asked Tom what advice he would give to kids who would love to appear on a Wheaties box. Dolan responded, "Don't strive for that. Strive to be the best in your sport and to be the best human being you can be."

How has Tom Dolan been able to manage this delicate balance between life, competition, and death? He loves to compete. He loves what he does. His motivation is so high that his breathing handicap, instead of serving as an excuse, became part of what motivated him to excel.

So often we talk about life in terms of a baby drawing its first breath and a dying person exhaling his last. Think about Tom Dolan for a minute. Why do we so often pay so little attention to all those breaths between the first and the last?

29

Monica Weidenbach

Celebrities and sports heroes certainly get a lot of media coverage and have a tremendous impact on those who admire them. But there is a special place in my heart for the quiet, lesser-known battlers that I see every day. They don't make headlines, but their lessons are no less powerful. One morning I was waiting for a plane and I read about a local boy who was playing on his high school soccer team. Nothing unusual? Well, this young lad was playing with a walker for support. I thought, "There must be thousands of folk like that, in every avenue of life, filled with personal, courageous stories."

Monica Weidenbach is one of them.

Monica was a high school English teacher in western New York. She and her husband, Ed, shared a passion for golf. "The first time I swung a golf club was in a crowded adult night school class. It was love at first whiff," she said.

It didn't take long for her to join in the quest of millions of golfers—take lessons to improve, get a hole in one, and make it to a twelve handicap. Monica's style was to respect her teacher, work diligently, and apply her never-give-up attitude. By the summer of 1997 she was golfing at every

Companions in Courage

opportunity. She joined a challenging local club and played so often that her Jeep could find the course in the dark.

But later that summer Monica began to feel some back pain after a round of golf. Aging? An illegal bag bursting with wedges? Not so simple. "The reality of my breast cancer in 1993 had returned with a vengeance. It had metastasized extensively throughout my liver, my skeletal system, and even to the marrow of my bones," she said.

The medical world presented Monica a grave prognosis with little hope. "I desired to live," she said. "I was forty-five years young, deeply in love with my husband, and filled with dreams, the least of which was to see my golf handicap in the low teens. When you believe you are going to die, it is not far-fetched to review your life, take assessment of more than your golf handicap."

Monica's life assessment led to an inward journey toward meaning and found its roots in a deep faith in God. She knew she was in a war. "I put on the whole armor of God and marched into battle and refused to even think retreat. Jesus was going to be my Companion in Courage," she said. Friends and loved ones helped carry the ammunition. Associates at her club established a fund-raising tournament for financial and emotional support. "It was less the appearance of a generous check and more the love of everyone involved that gave Ed and me the feeling we were not in this war alone."

Monica proclaimed her faith and believed that through God's love and his Word she would be healed of her cancer. Her style of playing competitive golf was a perfect fit for her battle with the disease. "I did not underestimate my opponent, but I did not allow his reputation to paralyze me. I knew about playing one shot at a time—now it was conquering one round of chemo drugs at a time, never looking too many holes ahead, and always believing in victory."

At the National Institutes of Health in Bethesda, Maryland, she found a healing environment on the cutting edge of medical treatment and also rooted in hope, compassion, and mercy. For a year and a half Monica traveled from Buffalo to undergo treatments. High doses of chemotherapy and other protocols were in themselves deadly, not to mention the grueling ordeal of a liver biopsy and various other medical tests. Because of a compromised immune system, she suffered through *E. coli* and blood staph infections that threatened her life.

"The details of what I lived through in those eighteen-plus months is not fit for print," she said. "That I lived through it is." And she continued to find solace in golf. "Sometimes, due to the medicine my feet and ankles were so swollen I could not get my shoes on. Ed would cut up my old sneakers and make a way for me to play."

Monica completed her clinical trial treatments in October 1998. Her faith had overcome the obstacles. Her courage was rewarded. The violent reactions to treatment, the loss of hair, the painful travel while sick, and the constant complications never dampened her faith. In fact, let it be known that she became the cheerleader for others at NIH and many relied on her faith and spirit for their own upbeat attitudes.

The fall of 1999 found Monica playing the game she loved with a renewed passion and outlook. She was golfing better than ever, her temperament milder and her competitive spirit more intense. She earned a spot on the club's Inter Club Team and enjoyed the sport in a way not possible before this all-out confrontation with a pernicious ailment.

Monica won many battles, but cancer eventually won the war in February 2000. Though she never felt comfortable with the label of "courageous," I saw it differently. Her faith refocused her life toward the promises of God, and her courage allowed her to follow them. At the funeral service, Monica's spirit of giving was everywhere. Most descriptive of her love for others were the words of her stepson: "For three days now I have listened to the words of those of you who loved Monica. I would walk around and overhear someone say, 'She was my best friend.' I would walk to another corner of the room and hear again, 'She was my best friend.' In the midst of her battle she made us all feel special to her."

SECTION 6

Standing
Tall

30

Aimee Mullins

Memorial Day. Washington, D.C. A Vietnam veteran named Phil Hebert stops Aimee Mullins. He removes his Purple Heart from his jacket and pins it on Aimee. Then he takes her hand and touches his skull, where the shrapnel still lies.

He tells her, "You have more courage than most people I know."

Aimee tries to refuse the medal but realizes, "This is what it's all about, this whole idea of being inspirational. This is just what I wanted to do."

The thought sticks with her through the evening.

"That night at dinner I cried and cried. This guy gives me a medal that is the symbol of courage and I look at us. Him, a guy who got shot in the head at nineteen, and me. And I think, We didn't ask for this. So is it because of courage that we go on? What else are we supposed to do? Give up? No. No. You don't give up till your heart stops beating."

Cool, confident, charming, and talented, Aimee might well have been viewed as another golden child, born to privilege and success. Today we know the qualities within her, but at the beginning the issue was what she was born without.

Legs have two weight-bearing bones, the tibia and fibula. Aimee, of Laurys Station, Pennsylvania, was born without fibulas.

For her parents, Brendan and Bernadette, the options were dire and direct opposites. They could let their little girl spend her life with deformed legs and webbed toes, or they could elect surgery to amputate their baby's legs just below the knees and replace them with prostheses. Even with the operation, there was no guarantee she would ever walk.

On her first birthday Aimee had surgery. At two she learned to walk with heavy, wooden artificial legs. She underwent several more surgical procedures when she was three and five and endured her last one at eight. She would stay in the hospital for weeks at a time, then undergo five to six months of physical therapy after each visit.

In this hard soil, the seeds of Aimee's spirit and uniqueness began to grow.

"The doctor would bring his medical students to my room just to see me do all the things they said I'd never be able to do and to tell them, 'Keep an open mind.'" She would have added, "And keep an active body." It was difficult to keep her in her wheelchair even during the months of her physical therapy because, as she puts it, "I hated that feeling of being confined."

As a kid she played kickball and tag with her brothers and some thirty cousins. Later she swam, played soccer, skied, and biked each morning to deliver the paper. "When she got up and started to go, there was no holding her back," her mom says.

The family loves to remember her first visit to the beach at age seven. Aimee, in her usual full-of-life spirit, charged right into the surf. A crashing wave sent her flying and she was driven underwater. When she surfaced, she had removed her wooden legs and tucked them under her arm. "I just kinda hung out that way, just floating," she says with a laugh.

Aimee never had time to think of herself as a victim. She would roughhouse with her brothers, take her licks with the rest. There was no coddling. Those artificial legs took an awful beating. "My parents didn't try to shield me from physical and emotional scars, which is why I'm not afraid of being wounded now," she remembers. "One thing I love my parents for was that I was never segregated or sat down as a little kid and told I couldn't do something. I'd just go."

While the world outside her home was not as understanding, Aimee was taught to turn setbacks into personal victories. In elementary school a teacher recommended home schooling because Aimee's presence was "improper" and "a distraction to the other kids." She was asked to have a monitor on a biking trip because they were afraid she might slow down the class and not finish. An elementary school gym teacher wanted Aimee taken out of her class because one day, as Aimee danced with a friend, her leg snapped in half and the other kids screamed. And, of course, she was teased about her "wooden leg." But Aimee always showed them what she was really made of. She finished the bike trip with the others, and one day for show and tell she just took off her legs, held them up, and said, "See, they're not wooden."

All of this made Aimee stronger. Her sense of humor and perky spirit helped her acceptance of the prostheses, and her attitude made things easier for others. "I used to enjoy jolting my substitute teachers by flipping a bolt and turning my feet backwards when they weren't looking," she recalls with a laugh.

To this day Aimee sparkles with fun and fantasy. "I want

to be a Bond girl. Think about it—I have metal compo-
nents in my legs, so when I go through airport security I
set off the alarms. But when they realize why I'm beeping,
they let me through. What if I had weapons in my legs? I
could take one off and pull out an Uzi! Legs Galore—that
would be me!"

In 1993 Aimee was awarded one of three full-ride college scholarships from the U.S. Defense Department and
matriculated at George Washington University. She had
never formally participated in track and field, but she became aware that just a few blocks from campus was one of
the most renowned coaches in collegiate track, Georgetown's Frank Gagliano.

Says Gagliano, "I received this call out of the blue and
frankly, I don't remember the details. I field a lot of calls,
but this was different." In his thick New York accent, "Gags"
recalls that twenty-fifth day of August 1995. "Aimee said that
she was a double below-the-knee amputee and that she
wanted to run track." He was deeply touched. "Fine. Meet
me at the track at noon."

A few weeks before the call, Aimee had run in her first
track meet. It was an event for disabled athletes in Boston.
She signed up for the long jump and the 100- and 200-
meter races. To her astonishment, she won all three.

While at GW she would run to Georgetown to work out
on the track and take a cab back to class. In January 1996,
Aimee transferred to Georgetown and became a walk-on
on the track team.

She competed in the 100- and 200-meter races in meets
where minimum times were not required to enter. At first
her times were slow and her stamina restricted by the extra
energy needed as an amputee. But Aimee was committed
to success.

"I really admire her," Gagliano says. "We worked her hard.

She wanted to work and to be good. When she came to practice I saw a young lady who had a heart of gold."

Further help came from Van Phillips, a single-amputee athlete who designs artificial limbs for athletes. He worked with Aimee to fit a pair of legs called "flex-sprint2s," made of extra-light carbon graphite that lock into the stumps just below the knees. Her feet, made of the same material, would hit the ground on just the toes. For traction, Aimee attached the spikes of running shoes onto the tips of her feet.

In April, her first meet with the new legs was the Duke Invitational. She lowered her personal best in the 100 to 16.7 seconds. A few weeks later at Villanova, Aimee confronted a different kind of challenge. The thick silicone sleeves that held her new sprint legs to the stump had slipped off because she was sweating. She begged Gagliano to scratch her from the 200. "What if one of my legs flies off during the deuce? The crowd would freak out," she pleaded.

She parodies her coach's response by tilting her mouth sideways and, in her toughest voice, saying, "Ya gotta run da deuce. Ya can't be afraida da deuce! If your leg flies off during the deuce, hey, it flies off. So what! You fall down. Put it back on. Then you finish the race. What the hell."

Privately, Gags always knew her goals and her desire to succeed. He often says, "You know, she's not like everyone else." That she isn't. She is the only disabled athlete to compete in NCAA Division I track and field. She competed in the 1996 Paralympics in Atlanta and holds records for the 100-meter and the long jump. She has been awarded the D.C. sportswoman of the year award for an athlete with a physical disability. She graduated with a degree in history and diplomacy from the Georgetown School of Foreign Service.

Aimee's life took a fascinating turn when she met Heather Mills, a competitive skier who had lost a leg in an accident. Mills was wearing a specially designed cosmetic leg, and

Aimee's first response was, "I've got to have those." Until then, Aimee's legs were rudimentary leg-shaped foam pads. She would spray-paint them to match her skin.

She could hardly contain herself when the technicians brought out her new legs. The lifelike silicone skin and the streamlined fit were almost real. Because she was getting a complete set, she could create a body design of her liking. She chose to be five foot nine with a seven shoe size and French toenails. That night Aimee painted her toenails for the first time, went out shopping, did a fashion shoot, and danced the night away.

Aimee's new legs also launched a modeling career. Two years ago she debuted in a fashion show for designer Alexander McQueen, and a year later modeled for Anne Klein, appearing in ads in *Vogue* and *Elle* magazines. "I didn't need these legs to feel complete, because I felt that before," she says. "One reason I want to model is to do projects that challenge people's idea of beauty and the myth that disabled people are less capable, less interesting. That we're asexual. I want to expose people to disability as something that they can't pity or fear or closet, but something that they accept and maybe want to emulate."

While modeling and preparing for the 2000 Paralympics, Aimee cofounded HOPE (Helping Other People Excel), a nonprofit organization that helps disabled athletes receive training and a chance to compete. She hopes to establish an organization to help amputees get artificial limbs, as well as to speak to women, host a kid's TV show, and on and on and on. As her recognition grows, so does the influence of her courage.

"Beauty," she says, "is when people radiate that they like themselves. You wouldn't want praise for having blue eyes, since you had nothing to do with it. Not having legs is a lot like having blue eyes. I'm not amazing."

31

Sam Paneno

Sam Paneno had found his place, his role. He had transferred to the University of California at Davis from Hawaii to play on the Aggies Division II football team, becoming the starting running back in 1999. He couldn't know his career would not last long.

The second game of the season, against Western Oregon, showcased his skills all too briefly. He scored twice and piled up more than 100 yards through regulation time, but the scoreboard showed a 33–33 tie at the end of four quarters.

The Aggies got the ball in overtime, and the first play from scrimmage was a routine call, one that had worked well all game. Paneno took the handoff and ran to the left side. It was his last carry.

As the tacklers unpiled and blockers left the scene, Sam lay injured on the field, holding his knee. It was a dislocated knee, something to which football fans have become all too accustomed. But this was different. The dislocation had severely damaged the artery behind the knee and caused a disruption of blood flow to the lower leg and foot. Irreversible damage had been done to the muscles and nerves. Sam Paneno's life was about to change forever.

Several surgeries allowed the doctors to restore the flow of blood to the lower leg, but further efforts to preserve the leg and foot were to no avail. Sam Paneno's leg was amputated below the knee.

The loss of the limb devastated his family and teammates. Sam, however, stayed centered. Family and faith brought Sam to a place in life that allowed him to accept and understand the way destiny sometimes unfolds.

The incident drew much attention from the national press, and I was touched when I read the meaningful quotes attributed to this young athlete. The best way I know to share the courageous attitude that contributed to his recovery is to share Sam's statements:

"It's good to go out that way. I felt I played hard, so to go out of my football career like that, it doesn't bug me that much."

"I have no bitter feelings. I got a chance to play football for a long time. A lot of people don't get that opportunity."

"Life is too short to worry about football."

"Why should I complain? They have good prosthetics."

"From day one, I've looked at it in the aspect of 'every day is a new day,' and I have already gotten on with my life."

"The media experience has been very nice. I'd like to get the message that it's not that big a deal."

"I'm actually fortunate in that I thought they were going to cut me off at the knee and I've got inches and inches of leg left."

"My family and God have been through a lot together. With so much love from God and everybody else, there is no way I couldn't look at this in a positive attitude because I've gotten so much support."

"I don't see this injury as hindering my recreational sports."

I know I go back to this theme quite often, but my hat's off to parents who work so hard to instill the values that this young man expresses. Sometimes the winning and losing become the highlights of a story, at the expense of the hearts of the warriors who play the game.

That is what touches us so deeply. Sam Paneno lost a leg, but not hope. I have gained a Companion in Courage.

32

Diane Golden

In 1990, at the age of twenty-seven, Diane Golden announced her retirement from the world of competitive skiing.

In 1982, while a sophomore at Dartmouth College, she won her first world title in competitive disabled racing. In all, she won nineteen U.S. and ten World disabled skiing titles. She was once clocked at sixty-five miles an hour—on one ski. In the 1988 Winter Olympics in Calgary, Diane won the gold medal in the women's disabled giant slalom, a demonstration event. She led an impressive U.S. Disabled Ski Team to eighty-five medals against eighteen other countries in thirteen disabled skiing classifications.

She was the best, and she was extremely proud of the voice her success gave her with sports fans and sponsors to view disabled athletes as just that—athletes. In 1986 she won the U.S. Ski Association's Beck Award, given to the best American racer in international skiing. *Ski Racing* magazine named her 1988 U.S. Female Alpine Skier of the Year, and the U.S. Olympic Committee named her Female Skier of the Year. Not disabled skier. Flat-out, Skier of the Year. In October 1997 she was inducted into the Women's Sports Hall of Fame.

Diane's story of overcoming adversity is without question one that would inspire anyone who grapples with the meaning of life. Diane's athletic excellence, love of life, perky sense of humor, physical vulnerability, and journey through the highlights of victory and depths of despair have given us a deeply personal look at what it takes to overcome. One of her pet peeves is the use of the word "courageous" when talking about disabled athletes, but there is no other word that can describe the manner in which she played the cards she was dealt.

Diane's parents owned a vacation house in the Canon Mountain ski area close to their home near Boston. At five years old she was on skis, and her exceptional ability was soon obvious. At twelve, walking through the snow to her house, her right leg gave out. The diagnosis: bone cancer. Her leg was amputated above the knee.

"Even before surgery, my first question was, 'Will I be able to ski?' When they said yes, I figured it wouldn't be too bad," Diane says.

Her accomplishments were an expression of her spirit.

"All of us on the U.S. Disabled Ski Team were missing one body part or another. For some it was a leg or two, others an arm. Some were paraplegic. We all became quite casual about body parts. We knew that the fullness of our lives had little to do with the form of our bodies and had a great deal to do with the spirit."

This attitude was tested again on New Year's Eve in 1992. A biopsy was performed on her right breast. She had cancer again and would require a mastectomy. Again, her sense of humor and positive attitude prevailed. "Considering what I had seen, losing a breast wasn't such a big deal. Sure, I'd be a little lopsided, but so what?"

A week later the doctor recommended a biopsy on the left breast because of some concerns in the report. "It's probably nothing," he said, using the same words as the first test. "Just to make sure." Diane grew to hate those words. The results came back positive, and a double mastectomy was scheduled.

Soon after that surgery, during an annual gynecological exam, the doctors recommended a standard surgical procedure for what they said "was probably nothing," and she awoke to, "We had to remove your uterus." How much is too much?

I include Diane as a Companion in Courage for many reasons, one of which includes my understanding of the dark place the mind can go when our physical well-being is threatened. Diane remembers, "For the first time the bravado of 'Hey, a couple of breasts, and they weren't that big to begin with . . .' wasn't working."

I know that feeling. I remember after my concussion in Buffalo how the pep talks to myself didn't work. My frustration intensified. Life seemed to be unraveling and the fears were increasing. I couldn't sleep at night and my mind became a very scary place to go. For Diane it was depression and a suicide attempt. She wrote:

> Do they laugh
> that they ripped her into half
> of who she was before?
> A gross game
> of tug-of-war. They made sport until
> she danced
> No more and laughed no more
> and dreamed no more Oh, the Great Gods'
> tug-of-war
> Whatever for?

When I write of Diane's courage, my words cannot always describe the full pain of the battle. Her therapy, her falling in love and marrying Steve Brosnihan, her dog Midnight Sun, and her return to the ski slopes are all stories within themselves. But the profound result of her loving and being loved have brought Diane to a place where she states, "I'm as happy as I've ever been. And this right now is more important—even in the eyes of those who care about me—than whatever sadness might someday come."

Most of us do not live as if death has called on us so often. It makes a difference in how each day is lived. To live with love creates a boundary of protection from the vulnerability of despair.

It's all downhill from there.

33

Zoe Koplowitz

I never thought of a vitamin pill as some sort of miracle drug. But then I heard about Zoe Koplowitz and now I'm a believer.

The funny thing is, taking the pill isn't what helped Zoe. Not being able to—that's what made all the difference.

At twenty-five, Zoe Koplowitz was diagnosed with multiple sclerosis. Physical frailties changed and complicated her life, but, like so many who struggle with this crippling disease, she carried on as best she could. A success in business, she was co-owner of a trucking company by the time she reached her mid-forties. She led a busy life but not one filled with physical activity. Vitamin therapy and a pair of crutches helped her through her daily routine.

All of the vitamins she took surely did some good. But one day in 1988, the vitamin pill she could *not* take forced her to reexamine her life. What happened? She choked on a vitamin pill.

Anger and helplessness overwhelmed her. So did disgust with her physical limitations. Enough is enough. She chose at that moment to conquer twenty years of subjugation by a disease. Where could she even begin to climb such a mountain? Believe it or not, Zoe chose the most outrageous goal possible. She began to train for the marathon.

This was not your typical training program. She did not need a watch for timing the mile breaks. Nor was speed of the essence or the purpose.

In 1991, Zoe ran in her first marathon—the biggest and best of them all, the New York City Marathon. What a thrill. While she finished last, some twenty-seven hours after the start, she brought courage and determination across the finish line. And it wasn't even the finish line anymore—it had been dismantled and cleaned up hours earlier.

I'd love to tell you that she improved with time, but I cannot, and it's almost beside the point. One year it took her more than an hour to get over the Queensboro Bridge. The reason—the marathon crew had picked up the carpeting and her crutches caught in the grating. Each year since her debut, Zoe's time has actually increased because of the crippling effects of MS, but so has her impact on the city of New York and the world of runners. Her indomitable spirit, incredible determination, and absolutely fearless courage continue to inspire.

She encourages others in their own efforts to come to grips with disabilities. She addresses classes in the New York City schools, especially in the poor neighborhoods, teaching others that they can live against the odds. Her philosophy, to those who seem to have a very limited future, shouts the message, "Triumph can come through self-acceptance and a reluctance to admit to boundaries set by others."

She is part of a Chemical Bank program called the Achilles Ambassadors. What an incredible example she is to both kids who are disabled and to others who are learning to be sensitive to the potential of the disabled. "Disabled people have the same needs, wants, and feelings as everybody else," she says. "They just move at a different pace."

Zoe's story epitomizes what Companions in Courage means to me. Those who achieve their potential by tapping their inner strength give not only to themselves but also to others. When we unlock our own spirit and potential, we want others to experience the same confidence. We are encouraged and blessed by one another. What a powerful magnet for human compassion.

Consider Zoe's run in 1993. A few miles into the race, she saw a woman holding a sign encouraging all Achilles runners. Zoe asked, "Who do you know in Achilles?" The mother pointed to her disabled little girl, two-year-old Meena. Later Zoe told the mother, "I dedicated this race to Meena."

She had all kinds of unexpected company as she made her way to the finish. A group of French runners saluted her with their version of "La Marseillaise." Mexican runners gave her roses and kisses of support. As she neared the end, dozens of runners from all over the world saluted and cheered her.

A final story that truly touches my heart represents the capacity fellow athletes have for one another. Grete Waitz, nine times the New York Marathon winner, wanted to add something to Zoe's effort by offering a medal to celebrate her long run. Since Grete's husband had run the previous day, she rushed back to the hotel to get his medal. "Jack won't mind," she said, "and we must have one to give Zoe."

The hour grew late, but Waitz and friends talked the crew out of tearing down the finish line. They threw together some flags and re-created the finish. The cheering and the chanting, *Zoe, Zoe, Zoe,* touched the hearts of the crew, who now went running to get their cameras.

Up the final hill came Zoe, crutches and all. Nearly a

hundred runners and passersby accompanied her. What a great moment—in sports and in life.

Zoe had once again fulfilled the message that hangs on a poster over her bed—"The race belongs not only to the swift, but to those who keep on running."

34

Haley Scott

The University of Notre Dame women's swimming and diving team bus pulled away from Northwestern University's campus in Evanston, Illinois, and headed out into darkening skies.

The weather worsened on that January day. The wind whipped the snow into blinding whiteouts and glazed the surface of the road with ice. The bus fishtailed to the left, then to the right, and finally turned completely around before its momentum pushed it over the edge of the road into a ditch, barely a mile outside of campus in South Bend, Indiana.

The first swimmer to climb out into the icy ditch was Susan Bohdan, a freestyler. The bus had turned upside down and its tires were still spinning. Susan couldn't believe her eyes. She had a momentary fear that she was the only one to survive the accident. Starting to climb back in through one of the shattered windows, she saw some of the others struggling to escape.

Inside, the luggage and her teammates appeared to be piled on top of one another. Bohdan found Haley and instantly knew she was seriously hurt.

Swimmers and divers emerged from the bus with scrapes,

broken bones, lacerations, head trauma. Help began arriving almost immediately. The women were taken to three hospitals in the South Bend area. The night became colder and more ominous when the reality that two of the Notre Dame swimmers hadn't survived the accident began to make its way from hospital to hospital. The grief and heartache, coupled with the physical wounds left by that tragedy, made January 24, 1992, a day the University of Notre Dame can never forget.

Haley had broken her back. Dick Rosenthal, the Notre Dame athletic director at the time, remembers Haley well: "You talk about courage. Unbelievable! I rushed to the hospital and found Haley, an eighteen-year-old kid from Phoenix, Arizona, discussing her surgery options with the medical staff. Her maturity stunned me. They are talking about exploratory surgery and the reality that she may be paralyzed for life. She says, 'Well, let's get going. What are we waiting for?' "

Haley Scott underwent two operations that night and early the next morning. In the first, doctors inserted two metal rods along the back of her spine, then grafted bone from her hip and ribs into the vertebrae area that was shattered. In the second exploratory surgery, the doctors hoped to find a blood clot that might have been causing her paralysis, without success.

For the next few days, Haley tried a zillion times to get her toes to move. She could not. But on the fifth day, with her mother standing by and encouraging her, she wiggled her toes. Her stunned mother screamed as Haley made her first move on the long road to recovery.

About a month later, Tim Welsh, the Notre Dame swim coach, was sitting in his office when Haley Scott walked in. He couldn't believe his eyes. He got up and hugged her very carefully.

Haley returned to the pool about ten weeks after the accident. However, she had to leave the water when it became apparent that the rods in her back couldn't withstand the pressure that her swimming stroke was putting on them. They began to bend, and finally broke through her skin, necessitating more surgery.

During the first operation, which lasted for two hours, the rods were removed. The second operation lasted eight hours and required the temporary removal of several of Haley's organs in order to insert new rods. The third operation straightened her spine. It too lasted eight hours. The ordeal of procedures lasted ten days.

Where did this swimmer from Notre Dame get such tenacity and determination?

"For a while I didn't think I would be able to return to school for the fall semester, but that is where I wanted to be," she said. "I wanted to be back with my teammates and my friends. The accident is something we shared in common and each of us survived it in our own individual ways. We became each other's support system. We learned from each other. I wanted to be with the people who lived that experience with me. Back at school is where I belong."

Haley Scott began reporting on the swim team's events for the school newspaper. She used a golf cart to get around the campus, but each night she would walk a little. Gradually she began walking to class and to swim meets.

She also found a different Haley Scott, a mature young woman attuned to the pain in the world around her. "I am much more aware of suffering and what people have to go through when their lives are turned upside down," she says. "When I hear about an accident, I think about the people involved and what they face in order to recover. I'm more aware."

Haley Scott is a courageous young woman who inspired me when I heard her story. The clarity of what she wanted gave her the motivation to accomplish her goals. The team's tragic accident, the loss of her teammates, and the challenge of her recovery remind us not to give in to the temptation to feel victimized and get caught up in self-pity and martyrdom.

35

Paul Binnebose

I've spent a lot of my life on the ice. I've seen a lot of great things and some that were pretty awful. I've had my share of the good and the bad. And yet, in all my years in hockey, I'm not sure I've ever seen or heard of the equal of what happened to Paul Binnebose as he trained for his shot at the 2002 Winter Olympics.

Binnebose and his partner (and girlfriend) Laura Handy, top competitors in pairs figure skating, were on the ice at the University of Delaware's arena on the morning of September 29, 1999. Paul lifted Laura above his head in a move that shouldn't draw any undue attention. But then Paul fell. He and Laura hit the unyielding and unforgiving surface with a crash that changed their lives forever.

The impact split his head open from his neck to his forehead, and he went into seizures at the rink before he could be taken to the hospital. To add to the horror, his mom was there with her video camera, taping the workout. Instead she got a horror show.

Once Paul arrived at the hospital, doctors set out to save his life and had to employ radical strategies to do it. With his brain swelling three to four inches outside his skull, they could find only one way to relieve the pressure—they cut from one ear up across the forehead and to the other ear, and then cut out a piece of skull above his eyes.

The chunk of bone went into a freezer at seventy degrees below zero, marked with his name, to be reattached later. The doctors packed his head in gauze and labeled that too: "No plate, no pressure." The exposed brain area was covered by only a thin layer of skin.

Paul doesn't remember suffering the fracture. Or the surgery. Or the eleven days in a coma. Or three more weeks spent unconscious, infections of the heart and blood, a collapsed lung, and pneumonia. Twice doctors brought him back from clinical death.

Not remembering differs from not knowing. His body tells him every day what happened, and he can't pass a mirror without seeing the awful results of that on-ice slip. The right side of his face is paralyzed; he wears a black patch over his right eye, an eye that tears incessantly and wanders. His muscle definition is gone, his arms and legs like those of a stick figure. The impact of his fall on the ice severed the nerves that control the sense of smell, and he will never regain it. His days involve intense therapy and training.

All of that work and pain centers on a goal. Some people, including his mom, think he should give up on it, but Paul refuses to stop aiming for the ultimate.

"Forget the skating? I've been doing it for seventeen years," he says. "It would be more selfish to stop. I want to make an Olympic team."

The 2002 Games would have been his and Laura's best shot. The pair finished third at the U.S. Championships in 1999 and made the U.S. team that competed in the World Championships that year. Now 2006 looms, if Paul can make it back. I find it hard to believe he laced up his skates in mid-January of 2000, three and a half months after he died twice. Doctors told him he could skate without his protective helmet in a year to eighteen months.

Don't tell Paul Binnebose about the odds against his and Laura's making it to the Olympics. Look at the odds he has already overcome and listen to the way he keeps himself on the emotional high road:

"Good things have happened. I didn't die either one of those times. I got rid of the pneumonia. I don't have to have heart surgery. I don't have brain damage. As far as skating goes, I don't think we will know that until I get stronger.

"It's never a good idea to sit around and say, 'Why did this happen to me?' I've been skating pairs for seventeen years and this is the fourth time I've ever dropped a girl. I fully intend to have great things come from this."

36

Sarah Reinertsen

Sarah Reinertsen remembers the night her dad came into her room to take her picture.

At seven, she did not understand much. But she knew she'd be undergoing surgery in the morning. She knew when she awoke from the anesthetic she'd be missing a leg. She knew she was scared. She knew this photograph would be the only lasting image of herself as physically whole.

Don and Solveig Reinertsen's daughter was born with her left leg considerably shorter than her right. When Sarah became a toddler, doctors fitted her with a brace. It served her well until she was approaching school age and the difference in the size of her two legs became more pronounced. After consultation with their doctor, her parents decided that it was in Sarah's best interest to amputate her left leg above the knee. Little Sarah cried uncontrollably.

The surgery was done in two stages. First her knee joint was fused. The actual amputation followed three weeks later. Sarah's leg was put in a cast to protect it and her from any damage that might occur in an active seven-year-old girl's life. Her grandparents came to help, which was wonderful for Don, Solveig, Sarah, and her brother, Peter, who was four.

Sarah's toughest challenge was staying indoors when she would rather have been playing in the snow. But she couldn't play with anybody. She just had to wait out that winter until she could begin rehab that next summer. And when rehab came, it began slowly. Sarah had to learn to walk, run, and skip all over again. A very active child needed to find a different way to be active again.

Because her family was athletic, there was always competition going on among the Reinertsens. Sarah had learned to swim when she was three. Her parents encouraged her, but, more importantly, treated her like everyone else. When she fell, they didn't make a big deal out of it. They waited until she got up and then they all moved on. "They never saw me as limited," Sarah says.

She remembers camping with her family at a cottage where life was spartan—no indoor plumbing, running water, or electricity. Excursions to the outhouse were an adventure, particularly when it was rainy and slippery. She'd walk, fall, get up, fall again, get up and fall again, eventually getting there feeling relieved and victorious. Those trips to the privy set the stage for what was to come as Sarah matured as a young female athlete.

In fourth grade the teasing began, particularly from some of the boys. This was a tough time for her because she didn't want to tattle but neither did she want to be picked on. Her parents helped her find a balance in making decisions on her own. Sometimes she told her teacher and sometimes she chose to handle it herself. She didn't like getting anyone in trouble; neither did she like being teased about having a different kind of leg.

Fortunately, cruel taunts made up only one side of the equation. Sarah's close, wonderful, and supportive friends, who made life very satisfying for her, comprised the other. She kept working, gradually learning to run again by the time she was eleven, and began participating in the New York State Games for the Physically Challenged.

This event provided more than competition. It gave her a sense of community, camaraderie with kids who had the same challenges. It was at these games that I first met Sarah. Her love of life, her friendships, and her competitive spirit impressed me. That hasn't changed.

Sarah participated in the New York games until she was out of high school, and the events put her in touch with two other people who became an integral part of her life and athletic achievement—Paddy Rossbeck and Dave Balsley. Paddy ran a support group for kids with missing limbs. Sarah loved the group gatherings because she felt bonded with the other kids. There was a lot of encouragement to dream dreams, set goals, and inspire one another to achieve them.

Paddy, who is an amputee, ran marathons. In her sixties and still going strong, to this day she is an important role model and inspiration to Sarah. Dave is Sarah's coach. He is a physical therapist who taught her how to run—leg over leg, not just hop and skip. He inspired her to begin training for the Paralympics, and, at age thirteen, Sarah went to her first national event. The result: She broke the 100-meter world record for women above-the-knee amputees.

When Dave hooked Sarah into this world of international competition, he helped her set a course that she has been pursuing ever after. Since the Paralympic race, which took place just six years after Sarah had learned to run again, she has set world and national records in the 100 meters and 200 meters. She set a world record at the 1998 New York City Marathon, completing the course in 5:52:38. She has finished four marathons, run the Adidas 12-mile Trail Run, run 17 miles in the Hood to Coast Relay, and continued her education. Currently she is finishing her master's degree in broadcast journalism at the University of

Southern California with the support of "The Swim with Mike" scholarship. She looks forward to training for triathlons and beginning her career as a journalist. She hopes to cover a six-day marathon that will be run across the Sahara Desert.

Sarah ran a marathon on January 1, 2000, in Hamilton, New Zealand. While most of the world geared up for Y2K, she prepared to begin the New Year doing what she loves—running.

The beginning of the race was uneventful, but at the three-mile mark her prosthetic leg broke. "I sounded like Chitty Chitty Bang Bang," she says. "I didn't know what to do. Do I stop running? Do I keep going? I have twenty-three miles to go and I have a broken knee! Wait a minute. I can't quit. I have to keep going, so I'll just have to approach this race differently."

She pondered her options for a moment. She was sure that she didn't want a DNF after her name in the record book. She made a quick decision: "I'll use the Galloway Method—run three minutes, walk one minute. The walking will be a challenge without a heel on my prosthetic leg but I'll do it."

She ran alongside a Texan named Rosemary. They encouraged each other because twenty-three tough miles loomed in front of them. It started to rain; Sarah was relieved because at least it would take the edge off the heat and slow down her dehydration. With ten miles to go, she realized she had a chance to break her own record.

At the twenty-mile mark she pulled away from Rosemary. The clanging of her prosthetic knee got louder as she picked up her pace for the next three miles. She was now drinking fluids and putting on Ben-Gay Gel from her waist pack. The rain stopped and the sun came out, making the last two miles a challenge, not unlike those trips to the privy when she was a little girl. She was hot, dehydrated, and alone. She couldn't cry—she was too dehydrated. She heard her own moans as she entered the stadium but they were deafened by the crescendo of the standing crowd's cheers. The cheering drowned out her own guttural cries and the clanging of her knee.

She circled the track, feeding off the energy of those who were there, finishing the race in 5 hours, 48 minutes, and 32 seconds. Sarah Reinertsen had broken her knee and her own world record, by four minutes.

"When I entered the stadium, I was spent. But as soon as I saw the crowd standing and cheering for me, I was no longer alone. It was a *Chariots of Fire* moment."

That evening, New Year's Day 2000, Sarah celebrated her victory, filled with gratitude for her family, friends, coaches, and fellow competitors. Later, while sitting alone, she gave thanks.

Sarah loves to run along the beach in Southern California early in the morning when the sun is rising or in the evening when it is setting. It is a lovely complement to the star moving gracefully across the sand.

37

Ronan Tynan

Martin Byrnes of the *Limerick Leader* newspaper in Ireland was working on a project when he heard a familiar voice on a TV talk show. Not being able to place it, he looked at the screen. He didn't recognize the face but the voice kept nagging at him.

Later that night, it dawned on him. The voice and face were those of Ronan Tynan, the highly successful track-and-field athlete he had met in 1983. Tynan, whom Byrnes hadn't heard from in fifteen years, had become a famous singer—one of the Irish Tenors. How had Ronan, Ireland's sole representative at the British International Amputee Games in 1982, become a celebrated singer?

Born with a strong voice and weak, deformed ankles, Tynan eventually made great use of both his strengths and his weaknesses. As a young boy, he did his singing on the family farm in rural Johnstown, County Kilkenny. He sang to the cows and believed that those tunes inspired his bovine friends to give more milk. With the encouragement of his father, Edmund, Ronan made the best of his handicap, but it wasn't easy. His ankles bowed out so badly that they restricted his mobility. He credits his father, whom he called "Da," for instilling strength and a determined spirit in him.

"He was determined that I make something of myself," Ronan says. "He helped me to understand the importance of living in the present. He taught me never to look back because you can't change the past, and never to obsess on the future because it may not come."

A serious motorcycle accident when he was twenty led Ronan and his family to a critical medical decision—the amputation of both legs below the knee. At the time of his accident, Tynan was studying physical education at the National College of Physical Education in Limerick, Ireland. When he returned to school, he grew more determined than ever to succeed. As the first disabled person admitted to the college, he felt an obligation to excel.

Upon his arrival, he got out of his wheelchair, balanced himself on his prosthetic legs, and walked up the steps to his dormitory. And his surgical wounds hadn't even healed yet! In seven months he was out of his wheelchair for good and literally leaping past all manner of boundaries. His artificial legs, however, could not handle the demands of his physical education and athletic interests. He knew he had to get better legs if he was to be competitive, but their cost went far beyond his economic reach.

His classmates took up his cause and soon raised the money he needed. He traveled to Belfast to be fitted, and the next "leg" of his journey was under way.

Ronan had always wanted to compete in track and field. Now he was ready. A year after his surgery he competed in the International Olympics for the Disabled and won medals in the 100-meter dash, discus, shot put, and javelin. In the next two years Ronan set fourteen world records, won eighteen gold medals, and captured the title of Most Outstanding Athlete in the World at the 1984 Paralympics in New York.

Because of his physical-education background and his athletic achievements, Tynan decided to take the next great leap and become a doctor. He applied and was admitted to Trinity College in Dublin. He earned his medical degree in sports medicine and to this day practices in Kilkenny, specializing in the treatment of sports injuries. His medical expertise and the inspiration of his own accomplishments make him a popular choice for treatment among athletes.

Ronan Tynan always sang, whether he was running in track meets, milking the cows, riding horses, swimming, or teaching. Music was a part of him, its rhythms a part of everything he did. When he got to college he moved his talents from the barn on the family farm to several of the local pubs, singing Irish folk songs. His cows had given more milk listening to Tynan's tunes; now his listeners were giving praise and offering him money. With their encouragement emboldening him, he entered a TV talent show and won the national championship. The contest was titled "Go for It," appropriate for someone with Tynan's energy, courage, and zest for life.

He found a great similarity between singing and athletic competition. "You must look at the voice as an athletic instrument," he says. "It's a muscle." And in his vocation and avocation he discovered a harmony. "In both medicine and singing you are giving. When I sing to people, put out my soul, it can touch people. It can be good for them. And they see you for who you are, not your handicap or your façade."

Ronan Tynan loved whatever he did—milking cows, riding horses, athletics, medicine, music—and neither his bowed ankles nor the loss of his legs kept him from pursuing his dreams. The challenge of his handicap became the motivation that drove him to do what was important to him. He didn't lament his plight; it went with him as he did what he loved. His didn't let the loss of his legs affect the creative expression of his energy.

Tynan loved to sing, but he had never had any formal

training. "To be honest, I hadn't a clue. I just liked listening to tenors. I didn't know what lyric tenor was, or a spinto, or anything. All I knew was that I liked the sounds I heard."

He decided to take voice lessons. And in 1992 he won the John McCormack Cup for tenor voice. As he aged and his ability to compete athletically began to wane, his music career blossomed. His Irish tenor voice opened doors. He was invited to perform around the world. He gave himself and his music and became an inspiration to people everywhere—handicapped and able-bodied.

In 1996, while he was tending to chores on his farm, one of his horses reared and kicked him in the face, severely damaging his nasal area. His athletic interests and his musical career were colliding. He had to have surgery to correct the damage to his face, but, with his usual drive, he tried to come back too soon. His next concert was a shattering disappointment—he lost his voice and his scheduled concerts were canceled.

The support of his family, friends, fellow athletes, and musicians kept him going. After a while he began to get his voice back and gradually began singing in public again. Two years later, in 1998, Ronan suffered another devastating loss—his beloved father died. In the hours before the burial, his voice failed him yet again. What to do? "The morning of the funeral, I couldn't sing a note," he says. "But at the funeral, I sang like a lark because I loved him so dearly."

Whether Ronan was losing his legs or his voice, his determined love of life and the support he felt from his family and friends inspired him to amazing achievements. A documentary about his life was titled *Dr. Courageous,* a fitting tribute to a man who didn't let his handicap or his setbacks keep him from a life much like a piece of modern music—highs, lows, some dissonance. But all in all, a sweet serenade.

SECTION 7

Defying the Odds

38

Vladimir Konstantinov and the Detroit Red Wings

Signing autographs was part of my life as a professional athlete. Seeing the excitement in kids' faces and sharing in their dreams gave me great satisfaction when I spoke with them and signed a stick or a puck or a picture for them. My next Companion in Courage left me with an entirely new appreciation for what a simple autograph can mean.

Two years after the Detroit Red Wings repeated as National Hockey League Stanley Cup champions, a child asked one of his heroes for his autograph. The writing was a little crude and actually hard to read. But with all the focus and energy that made him one of the best hockey players when he was on top of his game, he scratched out V-l-a-d-i-m-i-r K-o-n-s-t-a-n-t-i-n-o-v. He gave it to the fan with a smile. His wife, Irina, told the young boy, "You know what, maybe it's not the best signature, but make sure you tell all your friends you got the very first one." Just to be able to write his name was evidence of an amazing amount of courage.

Let's back up and set the stage for this.

Three years earlier, the Red Wings had celebrated a Stanley Cup victory. Captain Steve Yzerman skated the victory lap with the Cup over his head, passing it to Slava Fetisov and on to Igor Larionov and soon into the hands of Konstantinov. It had been forty-two years since the city of Detroit, steeped in the tradition of hockey, last laid claim to the Stanley Cup. Emotions ran high, and for a full week everyone felt like partying. The week of formal celebration was to end with a golf tournament.

Golf day came and brought perfect weather with it. The lone absentee was Igor Larionov. "The morning was sunny and warm, the best day yet, and my girls wanted to go swimming. How could I refuse?" Larionov said. "So I missed the golf outing."

Igor missed the tournament and more. Leaving the course, a limo, carrying three friends and teammates, headed home. The driver may have dozed off while traveling at high speed. The resulting crash left Konstantinov and team masseur Sergei Mnatsakanov in comas, Konstantinov for nearly six weeks. Their buddy, Fetisov, suffered serious chest injuries. It happened quickly, brutally, tragically. Of course it would never make sense, but we would all ask the same questions: How could this be? How do you explain it? Are there any answers?

For some, like Yzerman, the Stanley Cup victory suddenly didn't look so important next to life and death. "At the time, we were all thinking this is the most significant thing that could happen to us. Six days later, we realized it wasn't. It was definitely a strong reminder that playing hockey is not the most significant thing that can happen in your life."

For Slava Fetisov, history seemed to be repeating itself. Back when he was a star in Moscow, his younger brother,

Anatoly, had been killed in an auto accident. For Slava Koz-lov, the pain also raged intensely. When he was eighteen, he and a teammate had gone through the windshield of a car that crashed into a bus. His teammate died.

The Sunday afternoon following the accident, Father's Day, the Red Wings were in a hospital room, rallying around their friend. They filled the room with talk, Russian music, and familiar voices. They made sure to play "We Are the Champions" by Queen, the rock-and-roll anthem Vladdie had played over and over during the playoffs. That song filled Joe Louis Arena the night they won the Cup. The music, prayer, and friendship provided a springboard for a long year of hope made bearable by support from all over the world.

A Texas senator sent an authentic U.S. flag that had once flown over the capital in Austin. From the U.S.S. *Clark* came the captain's hat and picture of the crew. Irina was over-whelmed. "I cannot believe how much people send us— toys, teddy bears. But you know what brings the most tears in my eyes? The little kids who sent drawings from their heart, who write and say they pray every day for Vladdie. Those are the most amazing," she said.

After a winter of rehabilitation in Florida, Vladdie re-turned home in May 1998. His recovery time was spent playing chess, watching cartoons with his daughter, Anas-tasia, and playing tic-tac-toe with the kids in the neighbor-hood. On his better days he sat in a wheelchair, put a hockey stick in his stronger arm, and played in the drive-way. And how touching is this? Anastasia would often ask her dad how to spell a word for her homework. She knew how to spell. She was just trying to help him recover his memory. Children are incredible. I myself remember how my kids helped me through my struggles and what won-derful and bright-eyed cheerleaders they can be.

The Konstantinovs' positive attitude does not leave room

for bitterness. When asked about the limo driver, Irina says, "He is justice's business. A lot of people laugh at me, but I believe in justice in this country." They have balanced faith, hope, and the gratifying support and love from Vladdie's fans.

The driver, Rich Gnida, was sentenced to nine months in jail, fifteen months of probation, and two hundred hours of community service for driving with a suspended license. He later got hit with a ninety-day sentence for violating probation. But let's not talk about this part of the story anymore. Let me take you to Joe Louis Arena for the start of the 1997–98 season. It's October and time to celebrate the Stanley Cup victory one last time.

The opening ceremonies included the lowering of seven banners, slowly falling from the rafters. Each represented a Stanley Cup won by the Red Wings in their long and distinguished history. The crowd went wild. An eighth banner was in a box at center ice with the winged wheel emblem. The players were introduced one by one. Next, the names of the two men not present, Vladimir Konstantinov and Sergei Mnatsakanov, were flashed on the scoreboard. Former winger Mickey Redmond announced, "We know that Vladdie and Sergei are watching tonight. From all of us to all of you, come back soon. We love you. We believe."

Irina Konstantinov and Yelena Mnatsakanov took the ice to represent their husbands. The box was opened, and Steve Yzerman skated away with the Stanley Cup as the eighth Stanley Cup banner sailed toward the rafters. The seeds of a repeat were planted.

With the Wings deep in the 1998 playoffs and leading Dallas two games to one, Vladdie made his first appearance in Joe Louis Arena. Before the game, Irina recalled, "He shook everybody's hand in the locker room. I don't think he had any trouble recognizing everyone." The 20,000-plus fans greeted him with an overwhelming ovation. Just a few days later, on June 17, 1998, the Red Wings won the Cup again. As soon as possible they brought the Cup to Konstantinov. Kris Draper poured some bubbly in it and said to Vladdie, "Do you want a sip?" Konstantinov glowed with pride and appreciation. Draper and Chris Osgood went to his wheelchair and tipped the Cup to share the victory. A few seconds later Igor Larionov broke out with "We are the champions, we are the champions." Two days later, more than a million fans celebrated with a victory parade down Woodward Avenue. Konstantinov and Mnatsakanov rode together. The cheers were so loud and inspirational that Konstantinov, with the help of Fetisov and trainer John Wharton, left his wheelchair and walked a few feet across the platform, the first public view of his determined recovery.

Wharton spoke to the fans. "I don't think anyone has to be reminded where this group of guys was one year ago today. A team that's used to sharing a dressing room and sharing good times was sharing a waiting room at Beaumont Hospital. And while we shared that waiting room, we shared with you the belief, the faith, and hope that our two friends Sergei and Vladdie would recover. And because of you and your faith and your belief, this team found the strength to do the same."

Vladimir Konstantinov can walk with assistance but uses a wheelchair frequently. He pops in a few times a year to see the Red Wings and remembers the older players. He still has problems with short-term memory. Sergei Mnatsakanov recovered full use of his mental faculties, but his legs and one arm are paralyzed. He gets around in a wheelchair. He had hoped to return to his career but has been unable to do so. He too takes in a few Red Wings games each season. When the two men show up, they provide a tremendous lift because of their dignity and commitment to healing their bodies and minds, but they try not to call attention to themselves.

Sergei, Vladdie, all of the Red Wings, and their great fans proved something to me. We're not in this alone, no matter how great the struggle. We all have fans to cheer us on, if only we make ourselves able to hear them. We are not forgotten in our times of despair or suffering.

Strength, support, and love are all around. That's what ennobles us and enables us to reach for the stars.

39

Super Mario, Super Stars, Super People

I first heard of Mario Lemieux in 1982, at the start of my first and only season in junior hockey. He and Sylvain Turgeon were the two names that kept coming up as I ventured from the United States into Canada to play for Verdun, just five minutes from Montreal.

Mario played for Laval, and we engaged in quite a duel for the scoring title, a duel I would ultimately win. My club went on to win the championship (played at the Montreal Forum, no less) and I was named Junior Player of the Year.

Mario became the first player selected in the draft and went on to a brilliant career with the Pittsburgh Penguins. Ten years after we went head-to-head for the scoring title in juniors, we matched up again in the NHL, and Mario topped me. If all we had to consider were his achievements on the ice, I would still admire him.

But Mario succeeded because he did not let injuries drive him out of the game and because he had the guts to conquer Hodgkin's disease. When he beat me out for that NHL scoring title, he had just returned from an absence caused by cancer. Now what kind of strength does something like that take?

Mario's abilities helped save hockey in Pittsburgh, and his business savvy saved it again. My old friend and competitor owns the Penguins, having stepped in to buy a money-losing franchise and keep it from moving to another city. Mario did not grow up in Pittsburgh, but I'd call him a hometown hero. He combines heart, brains, and dedication. He was never a fighter on the ice, but he's a warrior in life.

To me, that's uplifting on every level. We set our goals and dream our dreams, but we cannot know how treacherous a path we must navigate. We never know how much strength we will need or where we will find it until we really look inside. That's what makes Mario Lemieux a Companion in Courage. Here is a professional athlete who is to be admired for the way he performed in his sport and how he conducted himself and triumphed over ill health.

So many fine athletes achieve similar greatness away from their particular game and leave me moved by their grace, their determination, their dignity. I'm awed by the way they marshal their inner forces and refuse to bow to pain or disease. Even though I'm sharing the stories of less well-known people with you, I do want to take a moment to acknowledge some of the great names in sports. They too are Companions in Courage. You probably already know about their struggles, but I want to salute them just the same.

I'm thinking of folks like Andres Galarraga. The Atlanta Braves missed him as he sought to recover from cancer, but he came back in 2000 with that same old smile. He swung the bat just like he had never been away, and you could see that the joy in him had never left.

I'm thinking of Ernie Irvan. Here is a man who nearly

died in an auto racing accident at the Michigan Speedway in 1994 and yet returned to win again. He closed out his thirteen-year career on that very same track in 1997, winning in his final race. After spending most of his forty years around racing, Ernie really didn't want to quit. But he knew the time had come. "I have two kids and a wife that mean a lot to me. The doctors told me that if I was able to drive my daughter to school that it was going to be a very pleasurable moment," he said. "This is something that I treasure."

I tip my cap to Alberto Salazar, the fine distance runner. Eight years after a disappointing fifteenth-place finish in the marathon in the 1984 Olympics, he came back to compete again for a place on the 1992 U.S. team. He changed his running style and his personal style, welcoming God and spirituality into his life while chasing out bitterness and frustration.

Maybe you don't know about Kevin Glover, the longtime center for the Detroit Lions and Seattle Seahawks. Back surgery could have ended his career, but he saved it by dedicating himself to, of all things, swimming. Fifteen NFL seasons, more than two hundred games, three trips to the Pro Bowl. And yet his teammates found more to respect in the bravery and intensity of Kevin Glover's efforts to return. All they had to do was watch him walk. "It's incredible that he's come back from that kind of injury," said Seahawks guard Pete Kendall. "You look at the scar and you just shake your head."

Scars? Monica Seles bears scars. As if defeating an opponent on the tennis court doesn't take enough concentration and energy, she had to overcome the stab wounds inflicted during a match by a knife-wielding "fan." Imagine the courage it took just to get back on the court. Flesh wounds close. Psychic wounds often require a greater strength, and I'm a Monica Seles fan because of her inner toughness. Same for Jennifer Capriati, who lost her way but managed to deal with her personal problems and make it back to the tennis tour. I'm also very moved by the plight of Chinese gymnast Sang Lan, paralyzed below the middle of her chest at the age of seventeen in 1998 after a fall during warmups for the Goodwill Games in New York. The attending physician, Dr. Vincent Leone, had himself been a high school gymnast. In comforting his young patient, he mentioned he had injured his back in his pursuit of excelling in the sport and decided to become a doctor. She told him, "Then I'll be a doctor too."

I could go on forever. Lance Armstrong beat testicular cancer, then defeated the best cyclists in the world to win the Tour de France—twice. He observed, "If I never had cancer, I never would have won the Tour de France. I wouldn't want to go through that again. But I wouldn't change what happened to me." Lance emerged stronger and showed us all that a killer disease can be turned inside out. Scott Hamilton also survived testicular cancer. The gold medal winner in figure skating at the 1984 Olympics, he now runs a program called CARES (Cancer Alliance for Research, Education and Survivorship). "My dream in my lifetime is that cancer no longer exists," he said.

I remember Houston Astros manager Larry Dierker suffering a seizure on the field in 1999. I had my TV on and watched in disbelief as his athletic body flailed uncontrollably in front of a shocked, silent crowd of 39,773. It took twenty minutes to bring him under control. Finally he lay quietly enough to be strapped onto a stretcher and rolled into a waiting ambulance. The crowd and Larry's players watched as he was taken from the field. He had a blood clot in his brain. Surgeons did their job well, and Larry Dierker returned to do his well too—in a month. "Having received so many cards and letters, knowing that people all over the world were praying for me, making donations in my name to charities, such a massive show of support made me realize how important what we do is to others," he observed. "I have a new appreciation for the precious things in life. This is the most important thing that has ever happened to me in life. I am blessed."

Aren't we all, even if at times it seems we are cursed? We don't win our wars without a struggle, and we don't always emerge unscathed. But we're here, alive, in this world, and we need to take all the good we can from that, even as we prepare to give back.

I think of jockey Chris Antley, beset by weight and drug problems, turning himself back into a well-conditioned athlete and winning the Kentucky Derby. I think of golfer Muffin Spencer-Devlin, fighting on many fronts against drugs, depression, and bipolar disorder, and surviving to help others find the proper treatment.

Sean Elliott. Here's a basketball player who needed a kidney transplant and returned to play in the NBA. And Roger Neilson, coach of the Philadelphia Flyers, who refuses to let cancer keep him from trying to get back behind the bench. Paul Stewart, a tough American in love with hockey, who made it both as a player and an NHL referee while defeating cancer. Cris Carter, whose NFL career nearly ended because of drugs, and whose spirituality and rebirth enabled him to ultimately become one of the finest receivers to ever wear an NFL uniform.

Few lives unwind untouched by difficulties and pain. We must face and fight what fate puts in our path if we're to get to the place we want to be. Isn't it just a little easier when we know that others have preceded us and we can profit by their example?

40

Gail Devers

As Gail Devers placed her feet into the blocks at the 1988 Seoul Olympics, her heart raced out of control.

But not because she was pumped for the start of the race. Here she was at the Olympics, with the whole world watching, and her life seemed like a nightmare. Her mental and physical strength kept ebbing away, other symptoms manifested themselves, and no one, least of all Gail, had any answers.

Some questioned her sanity; others wondered if drugs were her problem. She heard the whispers about whether she was starving herself with an eating disorder. Gail weighed a mere eighty-nine pounds and her hair had started to fall out. Her face turned an ashen gray. She felt increasingly desperate, even suicidal.

Gail had always been able to overcome her inner demons by pushing herself; this time she drove herself beyond all reason. Up until 1987 she had enjoyed good health, becoming a nationally ranked runner on the UCLA track team. The first signs of a problem occurred when her trademark fingernails began to break for no apparent reason. When her eyes started to bulge, her weight began to fluctuate, and her heart rate became erratic, her confidence turned to confusion and concern. Because she had set the world record in the 100-meter hurdles, her expectations, along with everyone else's, were high as she tried her best to focus on getting off to a good start that day in Seoul. But she was an emotional and physical wreck as the race began, and she ran nowhere near her best.

The "Alligator Woman," as she now called herself, returned home—terrified, depressed, and suicidally reclusive. Her coach, Bob Kersee, tried every conceivable diet to help his star athlete recover, but she continued to waste away. She stopped looking in the mirror because she was horrified at the sight of her scaly skin and bulging eyes. Gail didn't know it but she had what is called Graves' disease— an overactive thyroid. Gail felt a little better one day, so she decided to attend a UCLA track practice instead of staying in seclusion. Carol Otis, the UCLA team physician, almost fell over when she saw Devers. She told her she needed to have her thyroid checked immediately.

One visit to a specialist later, Devers began treatment. She began to take radioactive iodine to shut down her overactive thyroid and synthetic hormones to replace what the iodine destroyed. Gradually she began to recover, but not without a very frightening episode.

At one point, with her feet swollen almost beyond recognition, doctors told her they were contemplating amputation. Could there be a crueler irony for a track star? She refused to even consider it. In her own words, "I reached down inside myself, to find the inner strength to survive and run again."

In what seemed like an eternity, Gail Devers moved from a wheelchair to crutches and back to her feet. Her faith in God and the loving support of her family and friends enabled her to get her life back and return to the track. She made the U.S. Olympic track team and won the gold medal in the 100-meter sprint at the 1992 Barcelona Olympics.

She also ran in the 1996 Olympics, where she won golds in the 100-meter sprint and the 4-by-100 relay, and ran the 100-meter hurdles at the 2000 Olympics in Sydney.

"Everyone has obstacles to overcome. No matter how hopeless things may seem, never give up on yourself," she says.

On August 29, 1999, the thirty-two-year-old Devers set a new American record in the 100-meter hurdles at the World Championships in Seville, Spain. Her time of 12.37 was the fastest in the world in seven years.

The "Alligator Woman," who wanted to die because she was losing her athletic body and mind, survived despair because a champion's heart beat within her.

41

Jon Brianas

The winter wind coming off the Severn River in Annapolis, Maryland, puts a bite on the heart and soul, not to mention the flesh. It's one more test the lacrosse players at the United States Naval Academy must face as they prepare for their season.

Jon Brianas knew that all too well. He had gone to high school in Annapolis before gaining his appointment to the academy. As a senior in 2000, and as a team captain, he felt he could not shirk the responsibility of leading his teammates in their stretching exercises on the banks of the Severn.

He couldn't do it every day. It's one thing to fight that wind. It's another to struggle against a recurrence of testicular cancer.

Some days the weather and his fatigue just conspired against him. Other times, Brianas got out there in front of his teammates and amazed and awed them with his determination.

"Seeing him do that made us practice and play so much harder," said teammate Chad Donnelly, a defenseman. "He is our captain. We would follow him anywhere."

During the spring of his junior year, Brianas had seen

183

triumph fade into the gloom of illness. On April 3, 1999, he scored twice in a 12–11 overtime victory over George-town that clinched an NCAA tournament bid for Navy. Later, he told his roommates he had found a lump on one of his testicles. After a few jokes and some nervous laughter, Brianas saw a doctor. Surgery immediately followed, and he was expected to remain cancer-free.

He didn't tell many people about the operation, and he missed only two games. Then, in the NCAA tournament, he tore a ligament in his left knee and needed more surgery. Just before Thanksgiving, while playing football, he tore a ligament in his right knee. That injury might have been a blessing, for as he underwent presurgical blood tests, doctors found he had a low red blood cell count.

Testicular cancer's rate of recurrence is low, around 6 percent, but Jon Brianas had unfortunately defied the odds. Two days after Christmas, he began chemotherapy.

There were three rounds of chemo, each twenty-one days long. After the final series, near the end of February, Brianas arrived a few minutes late for a lacrosse team meeting. He could not believe what he saw when he walked in the door.

"The entire team had shaved their heads because they knew I had lost my hair because of the treatments," he said. "There are a lot of moments I will remember for the rest of my life. And that was definitely one of them."

Jon Brianas, puffing and wheezing and catching a chill, led his teammates in their exercises whenever he could. He missed five games, suited up but didn't play in the next, and then made his return to the field on March 29, 2000. In his return he scored a goal in Navy's 17–2 victory over Air Force.

"The first time I got a pass, it bounced off my chest, but we got it back," he said. "Then they moved the ball around again and this time I caught the pass and shot. Then I saw the back of the net move."

Midfielder Adam Borcz ran up to him and said the sweetest words any athlete making so difficult a return can ever hear: "That's the one. Now you are back. Now you are back."

42

Jim Morris

A deal is a deal. And what a deal Jim Morris made.

When the high school baseball team from Reagan County High in Big Lake, Texas, bargained with its coach, the boys knew it might be the only way they were going to stop him from pitching batting practice. They'd seen enough of his ninety-mile-an-hour fastball. So they negotiated. If the team won the district title, the coach would agree to go to a big-league tryout camp. Jim Morris, even though he thought he had no chance, agreed.

The team won the title. And in June Morris headed off to the Tampa Bay Devil Rays' major league tryout camp in Brownwood, Texas.

Now what are the odds of a thirty-five-year-old high school science teacher and baseball coach becoming a professional baseball player? Improbable? Yes. Impossible? Obviously not, because Jim became one of the oldest rookies to ever make it to the major leagues.

When Jim Morris took the mound for the first day of tryouts, he was so nervous that he could hardly hold the ball. He took a deep breath, doing his best to keep his heart from jumping out of his chest. Trying desperately to remember what he had been teaching his players about pitching under pressure, he stepped into his windup and let the ball go. His first pitch was clocked at ninety miles per hour.

Jim kept throwing strikes, at one point tossing twelve pitches in the ninety-eight-mile-per-hour range. The Devil Rays invited him back to the second day of tryouts, and his stunning success continued. Morris signed a minor-league contract and started his career with the Durham Bulls of the International League. After distinguishing himself there, he was called up to the major-league club in September 1999.

Royce Clayton stood facing the newest Tampa Bay rookie, thinking that this was his chance to break out of a hitting slump. In four pitches eclipsing ninety miles an hour, he was gone. Jim Morris struck out the first batter he faced as a major-league pitcher. His next stop was Anaheim, pitching against the likes of Mo Vaughn, Jim Edmonds, and Tim Salmon. Morris had an advantage against these guys—he had used their hitting videos to teach his high schoolers how to bat.

What a strange journey to the place he had longed to go. When Jim Morris came out of high school in 1983, he was drafted by the Milwaukee Brewers. Because of shoulder and elbow injuries he never made it out of Class A. He retired in 1989, went back to college, and ended up in Big Lake, coaching baseball and teaching chemistry and physics.

Well, the teaching career is on hold. The Devil Rays are so impressed with Morris, they are sending him to the Arizona Fall League. Doug Gassaway, who scouted Morris when he came out of high school, says that Morris has one of the best left arms in baseball. Big Lake's excitement shows itself in the school's new decor—Morris's clippings now cover the walls of Reagan County High.

Keep throwing strikes, Jim. Never stop pitching.

43

Michelle Akers

The player-coach dialogue went something like this:
"How much playing time can I have today, Coach?"
"Let's try forty-five minutes."
"Not good enough. I want ninety."
"What are you trying to prove? Sixty."
"Come on. Seventy-five."
"Seventy."
You know this can't be hockey. We only have sixty minutes, and when your skating time is cut back, it's the first step toward the bench.

This was Michelle Akers, hero of the U.S. Women's Soccer Team. Her sport was her life, but it was also killing her.

Think of her as Michelle Aching. She literally threw herself into the game and at the opponents. And she paid for it. The list of injuries included knee injuries ("Twelve or thirteen," she says, "I forget."), a few concussions, and three fractured bones below her eye. But her body spoke to her in even more serious ways.

For years the world-class competitor battled exhaustion. Early in her thirteen-year career, after the 1991 World Championships, Michelle was constantly drained. Migraines became a part of her daily life.

"I slept all the time," she recalls. "But I had no energy."

The medical diagnosis was "fatigue and lethargy due to the demands of her grueling schedule." Sometimes after a practice a friend would have to drive Michelle home and put her to bed.

"All my dreams rely on my physical ability and energy," she says. "Not being able to be active would change who I am, and that was extremely scary. My strength, my stamina, my energy, my self-reliance and independence—all gone. Nothing I had relied on in my past was there for me anymore."

Akers tried to hide the extent of her struggle. "It was like when you have those nightmares, and you know there's a monster in the closet. You know you should look, but you don't. So you continue to be fearful of the monster but you ignore it. That's how I was with this illness."

In 1994 the monster broke out. During a match Michelle became delirious on the field. She wandered around out of position. When the team left for halftime, she stayed out and someone had to get her. This time it couldn't be chalked up to a tough schedule. Finally she remembers saying, "I'm not just tired. I'm sick. There's something wrong."

She saw an internist and journeyed through a medical trial-and-error diagnosis. Four months went by. Then her problem got a name: chronic fatigue syndrome. Bingo. Relief. Something to tackle.

For the next two years Michelle began to listen more carefully to her body and her spirit. She began to change the messages that drove her to the all-or-nothing training programs and full-throttle performances. She learned to control her eagerness. On the field, Michelle willingly converted from the greatest striker in the game to the greatest defensive midfielder. She no longer roamed the opponents' penalty box and then exhausted herself in retreat. She followed a new rule: Walk when you don't have to run and jog when you don't have to sprint.

Off the field, she worked with Paul Cheney, a doctor she met through her study of her disease. He changed her diet, while the team doctor began a program of IVs of electrolyte replacement solution to enhance recovery after a game.

She sought a balance between the needs of her game and the desire of her spirit. The label of "trainaholic" had to go, and she had to alter her schedule. She needed to travel less, play more, pray more, and see the beauty of life as well as the beauty of a well-struck ball sailing toward the corner of the net.

Michelle committed to more honesty in her relationship with herself, others, and God. "I don't know how to explain it without sounding syrupy," she says, "but Christianity became my strength. It gave me peace of mind. As a Christian, you know that things don't happen without a purpose. You know that God is doing something and you've got to trust that. In fact the illness brought me back to him.

"I think the challenge is to take these difficult and painful times and turn them into something beneficial, something that makes you grow."

44

Jamie McLennan

For Jamie McLennan, a twenty-one-year-old rookie, signing with the New York Islanders of the National Hockey League brought his dream to the edge of reality. Stardom couldn't be far off.

As a free agent at the end of the 1996 season, Jamie began pursuing a starting role elsewhere in the league. Hey, change is good. And life was good for this quiet, laid-back goalie, who thrived on the thought of establishing himself in the game he loved so much. He was riding high in his athletic and personal life, but he would face something more frightening than a wicked slap shot from the point.

In May 1996 Jamie spent a night with what he thought was a gut-wrenching case of the flu. The fever and vomiting would not relent. Maybe it was food poisoning. Twice he visited the emergency room, and then checked into the hospital in Lethbridge, Alberta.

The attending physician monitored his condition carefully and ordered intravenous medication. A rash developed and black spots appeared on his arms and legs. The doctors, recognizing signs of a potentially fatal disease—bacterial meningitis—said, "We'd better call your parents. You might not make it." The symptoms of this disease that inflames the membranes around the brain and spinal cord were now advanced. By the time Darlene and Stuart arrived, Jamie was fighting for his life.

Standing in front of the net and being blitzed in a 9–0 shutout would be mild compared to the next five days of head-spinning delirium and a raging fever. Jamie was so drained that when the fever finally broke, it was days before he was even able to manage a few steps without a walker. His eyes were sunken and puffy and his flesh had a yellow tint.

"I'll never forget how I looked," Jamie remembers. "Like it wasn't me." But he began to recover. His positive attitude, his sense of humor (the nurses told his parents he never stopped joking throughout the ordeal), and his dream of returning to the game he loved fueled his recovery. After what Darlene describes as "a dreadful, dreadful few weeks," Jamie returned home to Edmonton. He had lost thirty pounds and literally had to teach himself to walk again.

I remember so clearly the helplessness and frustration I experienced in my own recovery. I had always been able to do what I wanted. To be reduced to such an out-of-control state truly challenged my capacity to cope. Though Jamie endured a great deal of pain, his mind was clear. With so much time on his hands, and so little he could actively do, he contemplated and sorted out life and death.

"I learned not to take anything for granted," he recalls. "I can get out of bed in the morning. I wasn't able to do that when I was sick. When I was in the hospital there were kids who were sick and dying. I just think we're very fortunate to have our health."

Just two months into his recovery, in July 1996, the St. Louis Blues signed Jamie as a free agent. With training camp so close and his rehabilitation still ongoing, he did not have the strength to beat out veteran Jon Casey for the backup spot on the roster behind Grant Fuhr. He spent the 1997 season with the Blues' minor-league affiliate in Worcester, Massachusetts. He played well and was ready to put his name on the 1998 roster for the parent club. But another obstacle blocked the comeback path.

Earlier in the summer, the Blues had signed free agent Rich Parent to be the backup to Fuhr for the 1998 season. They penciled McLennan back at Worcester for another season. But Jamie had worked too hard to allow that. He beat out Parent and Brent Johnson for the backup role behind Fuhr for the 1998 season. He was solid. His 16-8-2 record and 2.17 goals-against average, accompanied by his two victories over the Dallas Stars, told the world he'd come all the way back.

His relentless approach and gutty performance throughout the year won Jamie the 1998 Masterton Trophy, an award for the player who exhibits perseverance, sportsmanship, and dedication to hockey. He proved his ability, character, and commitment to excellence. I am proud to have him on the list of Companions in Courage.

Jamie McLennan, sick as he was, could have spent his time singing the blues. Instead he impressed the heck out of the Blues and all of us.

SECTION 8

Escaping the Darkness

45

Seymour Knox

My success in hockey has opened doors and given me opportunities for which I am grateful. When I was asked to go see Seymour Knox III when he was very ill near the end of his life, another special event took place. When the last game was played in the Buffalo Sabres' old arena, known as The Aud, the organization wanted the closing to be memorable. Sure, Marine Midland Arena would have all the amenities the old building lacked, but it would not have history or Seymour's presence.

Everyone knew that Seymour, the team's owner, would probably not make it to the celebration because of the advanced state of his illness. As I sat with him that last time, he held my hand. We both had tears in our eyes, and he talked about how much he was going to miss not being there. Seymour had talked to his wife, Jean, about putting his initials on the new jerseys as a way of being with the team even after he was gone.

I felt very fortunate to play in that last game. We beat Hartford 4–1, and after the game, three players—one from each decade of the Sabres' history—took the puck and skated it around the rink. They waved to the crowd and shot the puck into the net. It was a high honor for me to be chosen to shoot the last puck. I skated around the rink, stopped in front of the net, waved to the crowd, and shot the last puck in the net. The whole building went dark except for a spotlight that illuminated the puck.

Emotions ran high for everyone in attendance that evening, whether on the ice or in the seats. Farewells are like that. I felt as though I was waving and saying thank you on behalf of all of the players to the great building and to all the fans who had supported the Sabres for over thirty years. Seymour, in one of his last speeches, had referred to The Aud as an old friend he was saying good-bye to. The Aud had been like a friend to all of us. I'll never forget him sitting behind the bench during every game wearing headphones and listening to the radio and watching at the same time with Jean beside him. He loved the game. And he loved the players like we were his family.

After I shot the puck in the net for the last time, I made sure one of the guards grabbed it so the players could give it to Seymour at the end-of-the-year dinner party. Kenny Martin, a good friend of mine who works in the office, was able to put together a nice plaque that read, "Farewell Old Friend." It was our way of saying the same thing to Seymour. We gave Seymour the puck mounted on that plaque. That puck was very special to Seymour. And that's what made Seymour so special—the little things in life meant so much to him. Friendships, compassion, caring, the gifts, and all the people who had supported the Sabres meant the world to him. That puck expressed how we felt about him and the old Aud.

I remember him holding my hand before he died and saying proudly to his wife, "Show Pat where I put the puck." I hugged Seymour and told him that I and all the players loved him. Jean took me into his favorite room and there, by his favorite chair, sat the plaque with the puck. Three years later, at my retirement party, Jean presented me with that puck and said, "Seymour would want you to have this." And I have it hanging up in my office.

When I read Mitch Albom's moving book *Tuesdays with Morrie,* I thought very much about Seymour. Seymour and I loved the game of hockey and even though our social and life circles were different, we were able to connect with each other on a very deep level. We had a desire to care and express our compassion for others. We talked about how we felt blessed and how we wanted to be a part of the community and give back to it in genuine, helpful ways. I felt very fortunate that I was able to mean that much to a man like Seymour. He had told me that he thought of me as another one of his sons.

Recalling my relationship with Seymour filled me with gratitude. I was also grateful to my psychologist, Ernie Valutis, and the doctors at the Mayo Clinic for their work that helped me return from the darkness of depression, enabling me once again to see the good things in life and to savor them fully. Getting to know Seymour in that time before his death, feeling his love and compassion for me as a human being and simply being with him at his most vulnerable times before he died, remains a part of me that I cherish deeply.

I remember him holding my hands and telling me his thoughts about death and life. He wanted to have a happy funeral and he wanted everybody not to worry. Even though he had withered away and the cancer had eaten away at him, his spirit was vibrant and alive. In his book about Morrie, Albom wrote of how he picked up his old and ailing college professor to move him to a more comfortable position. I did the same with Seymour. I'll never forget lifting him up and seeing the love, confidence, and trust in his eyes. And I'll never forget the spring day that Jean called me to come and visit him. She told me that Seymour wanted to see me Sunday if I could come. She told me that he was ready to see me because he was going to die soon. He passed away that Wednesday.

Speaking at Seymour's funeral proved to be one of the hardest things I think I ever had to do. I sat there listening to his son speak and I felt very honored that Seymour included me like a son after so many years of his life and the many acquaintances and many people he knew. I feel fortunate that he chose me and I feel lucky that our paths crossed.

Things do happen for a reason. I believe that one of the reasons I was brought to Buffalo was to meet Seymour and to know him and Jean. That friendship changed my life dramatically. Seymour was a professional owner who had millions of dollars but drove an old Mercedes that he had kept for years. Humble, casual, innocent, and shy at times, he was not afraid to be himself. You would never know his family had founded Marine Midland Bank. I think it was remarkable that in the midst of all that surrounded him, he was able to keep that inner, gentle, caring, and compassionate person intact. He touched everyone and everybody.

To me, there's only one unhappy element of knowing and respecting people like Seymour Knox. When they're gone, you miss them even more.

46

Cam Neely

The loss of my childhood friend John Brown, as well as my relationship with Erik Fanara, helped me realize how much loss can challenge and test us, even those who are tough and strong. Cam Neely, who played forward for the Boston Bruins, learned to reach down and find that inner grace as death touched his personal and professional life.

When he retired from hockey in 1996, Cam proudly carried the well-deserved reputation of a superstar who epitomized the balance between intelligence and physical strength. Yet the circumstances of his life on and off the ice pushed him to the edge of his capacity to cope. The combination of hockey injuries and the loss of his parents to cancer demanded all of the emotional strength he had. Both of these experiences forced him to change his approach to the game and to life.

Neely's hockey career changed dramatically on May 5, 1991, when he collided with Ulf Samuelsson of the Pittsburgh Penguins. The bruise from that blow was deep, causing his thigh muscles to calcify. The condition required surgery and a lengthy recovery.

Cam approached his two years of rehab with the same vengeance that he displayed on the ice. He persevered through a demanding exercise regimen and returned to score fifty goals in forty-four games. In March 1994 his comeback received another setback when he tore the medial collateral ligaments in his right knee. More surgery followed, but Cam bounced back and played two more seasons.

It seems so easy, in the space of a couple of sentences, to sum up what Cam went through. But as a professional athlete who has coped with injuries, I know just how exasperating it is to show up for rehab day after day when your teammates are on the ice, doing what you love to do and cannot. Cam gutted out ninety-three more games, relying on the intelligence and savvy that always characterized his game, to score fifty-three more goals. An arthritic hip finally forced him to retire on February 21, 1996.

Now let's go back nine years. That's when Cam's mom, Marlene, died of stomach and colon cancer. The year before, his father, Mike, a twenty-two-year veteran of the Canadian air force, was also diagnosed with a cancerous brain tumor and began radiation treatments. There's an emotional load that can crush a person in a tidal wave of grief. But Cam's heartaches pushed him to compete more intensely and ultimately helped him deal with his injuries.

When he was tempted to get down, he thought about the battles his mom fought and that his dad was fighting. He knew his dad would never quit battling.

When Cam was fifteen and away from home for the first time playing junior hockey, he wanted to quit. As the youngest player on the team, he felt totally out of place. Miserable and desperate, he told his dad he wanted to give it up. Cam's dad was not one to push his son, but he could make an effective point very quietly.

"My dad never told me what to do. He told me things, gave me his opinion, and then let me decide," Cam says. "When I told him I wanted to quit, he told me that I had signed a commitment and given my word. He told me that

I could quit if I wanted but he thought I should honor my commitment and be a person of my word. I stayed."

That mentality and the strength Cam drew from the fortitude his parents showed became the underpinnings of a new work ethic. He started what would be his last season with his old fire but pushed his knee beyond its limits. It ballooned on him and left him as depressed as he was when he injured it the first time.

He rested the knee and the swelling came down. He reluctantly accepted the pattern of his off-season practices—play, rest, play, rest—missing some games, babying the knee, working on the muscles around the knee, and playing like an all-star when his knee cooperated. With the soft touch and fluid skating style that always created the room he needed to score, he averaged a goal a game. He surprised everyone, including himself, excelling during the games without practice.

His dad came to visit in November 1993 to see his son play. He loved to visit, hang out with the team, and be with his two sons, who were now living together in a Boston suburb. After Marlene died, Mike had come more often and would stay a couple weeks each time. He knew in his heart that this November visit would be his last.

The doctors had stopped their treatment for the brain tumor, saying that there was nothing more they could do. Mike, Cam, and Scott knew what lay ahead but banished gloom from their little kingdom. They joked and laughed like old times, reveled in one another.

The day before he was to head home, Mike got sick. He checked into the hospital and died that evening. Cam and Scott accompanied their dad's body back to Maple Ridge, British Columbia, for the funeral and said a solemn goodbye to the man who had inspired them with his words as well as his example.

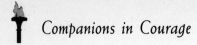

"I not only lost my father, I lost my best friend," Cam said.

Cam took many hits on and off the ice. He dug pucks out of the corners and he dug himself out of the personal corners of death and injury. He turned his setbacks into sources of determination and inspiration. Cam is a super-star not just because of his hockey skills but also because he persevered through his personal and professional challenges. Even winners suffer losses. It's what they do next that makes the difference.

47

David Duval

The stories of John Brown, Erik Fanara, and Cam Neely show us how death pushes us to the edge of our capacities to cope. We can be crushed by the weight of such losses. However, we can learn how to turn our losses into sources of determination to live our lives more fully, to reach our goals, and to pay tribute to those we have lost by giving back to those in need.

Learning to recover from personal loss is easier said than done. David Duval's story illustrates the difficulties of conquering the heartache of personal tragedy.

When David's older brother, Brent, was twelve, doctors diagnosed him with aplastic anemia. It is a disease that causes the bone marrow to stop producing white blood cells. He would need a transplant. The marrow would have to come from Deirdre, the boys' younger sister, or from David. David's marrow was a 90 percent match with Brent's. The doctors would draw marrow from David's bones by inserting large stainless steel needles six times into both sides of his pelvic area. Bob Duval still hears the scream that came from David when that first needle plunged into his son's hip.

The bone marrow transplant seemed to have worked,

and the Duvals hoped for the best. Then, as they enjoyed dinner out one night, Brent began to vomit. A few days later he had diarrhea and then developed a high fever. He had graft-versus-host disease. David's bone marrow had begun attacking Brent's body, and bacterial infection consumed it, one organ at a time.

Brent went to the Cleveland Clinic for treatment. It was the last place David would ever see his brother alive. Just as disease ravaged Brent, guilt ate up David. At the young age of nine, David felt sure he had killed his brother. Picture the torment of his parents, already grief-stricken, as they tried to comfort a surviving son who continually told them, "I killed my brother."

David had been a good-natured kid. He loved life, playing golf with his family at the Timuquana Country Club, and finding snakes and turtles around the ponds on the course. When Brent died, everything changed. David dropped into a deep place inside himself and developed his own personal routine of survival. He came home from school, dropped his books off without a word, and rode his bike to Timuquana. He'd get a hot dog at the concession stand and then go practice and play golf for hours. He loved playing in the fog because it protected him from whoever might be around, hid him and his misery.

At home, sympathy grew harder to find. Bob and Diane were living apart now. Their grief had pushed them away from each other. Like David, they coped in private ways.

Unlike his mother, David buried his emotions. Everyone noticed how reclusive he had become, but no one knew how to reach him. At night Diane would come into David's room and quietly caress his back, his head, and his neck to help him fall asleep, but David grew more stoical and hardened as time passed. His comfort came not from people but from his game.

Hammering golf balls on the range became his escape

and the way he steeled his resolve to win. He had no time for banter, parties, or hanging out at the mall with other kids his age. He maintained his friendships with several of his non-golfing friends but eventually went to a private high school and rarely saw them anymore.

When David reached age thirteen, he began to hit the ball longer and straighter. He started winning the club members' money and becoming more determined than ever to excel at golf. It was the perfect game for him because everything depended solely on him. That's the way he lived: Count on no one, let no one in. His shell grew thicker, his resolve to make the PGA Tour even stronger.

When someone asked him about his success, he replied, "To really improve you need to rise and fall alone, and each time learn why. That can be very lonely, but I'm not afraid of aloneness. I've done it. It's not so bad."

After graduation, David left home. He packed his clothes, his golf clubs, and his brother's Lamborghini poster and headed for Georgia Tech. His first day on campus, an upperclassman, Mike Clark, told David that the team was glad they now had a good fifth man on the team. David replied, "If I come here, I won't be Number 5. I plan to be Number 1."

In his first ACC Tournament David took second and the team placed fifth. When his teammate Tripp Isenhour complimented him on his round, David replied, "Yeah, and if I had teammates who were worth a shit, we'd have won the damn tournament."

Puggy Blackman, Duval's coach at Georgia Tech, is the one man who was able to see through David's hardness, to see a softness buried deep within him. David was so obnoxious that Puggy felt like he had two teams at Tech—David, and everybody else. David seemed to have no idea what camaraderie would do for him. He just kept building his inner wall higher and thicker. At one point Puggy called

Bob Rotella, a sports psychologist, out of desperation. Not much changed, so Puggy resigned himself to the two-team concept. "It was the only way to keep them from killing each other," he said.

The trips where Puggy and David ate and roomed together apart from the rest of the team began the process that eventually helped David emerge from behind the barriers that protected him from his childhood pain. Puggy talked to David about life, people, and the bigger picture of a spiritual design where everything happens for a reason. David listened to Puggy because he respected him, but his own sense of the way the world works remained deeply rooted in the death of his brother and the demise of his family.

If David leaned on anyone for support, it was a character in Ayn Rand's novel *The Fountainhead*, Howard Roark. Roark, an architect in the novel, believed that a man must maintain the virtue of a healthy selfishness. To have integrity, a man must serve his own ego and its truth. David read passages from the book over and over again and found a justification for his thinking and approach to life: "The basic need of the creator is independence. The reasoning mind cannot work under any form of compulsion. It cannot be sacrificed or subordinated to any consideration whatsoever. To a creator all relations with men are secondary." Duval loved it when his friend Kevin Cook referred to him as the Howard Roark of golf.

And yet David loved spending time with Puggy, his wife, Gail, and their three kids. Puggy felt like the shepherd trying to bring a lost sheep back into the human fold. His persistence would eventually pay off.

When Duval left Georgia Tech, he failed to make the cut at the PGA qualifying school. His mother was drinking heavily, trying to cope with her continuing grief, and his father refused to face what was happening. David became more distant, but a different sort of numbness was setting in. His

Roark-like strength drained from him. One week folded into the next; his golf began to slip. He was finishing way behind the leaders, and then he started missing cuts. Out of desperation he called Puggy. He was ready to listen.

Puggy talked. David listened. The message was simple: "Relationships are important and life is not just about you." Puggy was shocked and overjoyed when David agreed to accompany him to a College Golf Fellowship, a Christian gathering. Duval emerged from that experience with a new fire and played well enough to make the Tour.

Still, his acceptance of Puggy's faith and philosophy came slowly at best. David steeled himself against his pain and the people who had brought him this far. But Puggy knew that if David didn't soften his stance, he would not achieve the greatness of which he was capable. Deep inside, David now began to see it too.

Ever so gradually, David softened. He began talking to his father again and accepted the new woman in Bob's life. He started to face his mom's drinking problem and found ways to help her. What brought a smile to Puggy's face was that David began to make more friends and take time to go skiing and fishing. He began dating a young woman named Julie McCarthy. He began to feel again. Children with life-threatening diseases touched his heart. He couldn't believe it when he heard that a man wanted to be buried with a golf hat David signed for him. He lost weight and began spending more time out from behind his well-constructed wall.

When David won for the first time on the Tour, Puggy likened his experience to giving birth to a twenty-pound baby.

David spent so many years trying to protect himself not only from the outside world but the pain inside. The answer wasn't to keep others out. The answer was to let them in and let himself out.

48

Julie Krone

Judy Krone was selling a palomino to a woman who wanted a horse for her young daughter. She instinctively picked up her own daughter, Julie, and put her on the horse to show it was gentle. The horse trotted off and Judy said, "There, you see?" When the palomino reached the fence, two-year-old Julie instinctively reached down, took the reins, and nudged them into the horse. The horse trotted back to where the two women stood.

Judy was shocked by what Julie had just done but not really surprised by her baby's horse savvy.

Judy Krone had been raised in a very strict Baptist home and learned to look inward to find freedom. She lived in an imagination fueled by books—books about horses. Horses became her passion. When she became pregnant with Julie, riding helped her cope with the emotional and physical ups and downs. The thought of a miscarriage didn't enter her mind. Judy Krone was a champion equestrian rider. She loved horses and everything associated with the stable. Her daughter became an extension of that love.

Julie's childhood in tiny (population 494) Eau Claire, Michigan, had the look of an uninhibited free-for-all, but the constant was horses and her dream of being a jockey.

It was not unusual to find Julie eating out of the same dish with her horse and her dogs. One day she walked the horse in through the back door, past the kitchen and to the dining room, where her mother was sitting. An emergency? Maybe to Julie. She needed the horse saddled.

Julie lived on the edge. If she wasn't riding to school, hanging on to the bumper of the bus as it traveled over ice, she was standing on the back of a galloping horse and ducking under the doorway when it reached the barn. Don Krone, Julie's father, remembers life with Julie this way: "Every day was a missile launch. Yes, there was always that element of possible disaster, but it was just like a missile. If it goes, God, there's going to be that moment of glory. You can't tell a kid to go for it, to be whatever they want to be, and also tell them to be careful. If we all ride the safe road, who will we look up to? No, we didn't worry about the little things."

Julie and her mom attended every horse show they could, and the desire to be a jockey burned in her young soul. She entered and won a Youth Fair horse show at age five. Sometimes at night they would ride together, mother and daughter, singing above the mesmerizing rhythm of beating hooves.

In order to pursue her dream, Julie dropped out of high school and went to Tampa to live with her grandparents. When she arrived at Tampa Bay Downs to begin her career as a jockey, there was one problem—they wouldn't let her through the gate. Not to be deterred, the four-foot-ten-and-a-half-inch, hundred-pound girl climbed the fence and made a beeline for the barns. When she finally connected with Jerry Pate, a trainer, he said, "So, I'm told you want to be a jockey." Julie didn't hesitate: "No! I'm *going* to be a jockey!"

Five weeks later, Julie sat in the winner's circle. She won

nine races, had four seconds and ten thirds in her next forty-eight mounts.

Tampa Bay Downs trainer John Forbes describes what Julie faced as she made her way up the jockey ladder: "You've got to understand. Nobody took girl riders seriously—they were a joke. Nobody thought a girl was strong enough. Nobody wanted to be the one to get a girl hurt and nobody worried that a girl might beat him. It ate Julie up, to be considered a girl jockey. I introduced her to someone as 'jockette' and she kicked me in the shins."

Life was a constant battle. Fights with male jockeys, an estrangement from her mother, no high school diploma, a broken back in 1980 and four months of rehab—all these only intensified her determination to realize her dream. In 1982 Julie won the riding title at Atlantic City. She beat every man there and established herself. They now had to take her seriously. Two months later she won two races at Pimlico, and in 1983 she won the Atlantic City title again.

Jump ahead three years. It's 1986. Julie answers the phone and her mother's quivering voice announces that she has been diagnosed with cancer. End of estrangement. And even more reason for Julie to ride and win—to give her beloved mother a reason to live.

In 1987 Krone became the leading winner at Gulfstream Park, Monmouth, and the Meadowlands. She excelled as a jockey and in 1989 had her best year, winning 368 races. But her greatest accomplishment was still to come. She rode Colonial Affair to the winner's circle in the 1993 Belmont Stakes, the only woman to win a Triple Crown race.

Three months after her Belmont win, Julie Krone lost everything. Or almost everything. Riding Seattle Way in her third race of the day at Saratoga, she neared the top of the stretch and seemed poised for a winning charge. Then the horse beside her suddenly veered into her path, throwing her violently to the ground. Her legs twisted beneath her as she landed on her bottom in the path of a charging horse, who struck her in the chest and catapulted her onto another part of the track. She screamed in pain along with fellow jockeys Richard Migliore and Chris Antley, who fell nearby, the three a mess of sprawled limbs.

Julie spent eighteen days on a morphine drip. She survived two surgeries to repair her badly damaged ankle. Her punctured elbow and the throbbing cardiac contusion in her chest required constant monitoring.

"I went through a real bad depression," she says. "The pain ate at me. For two weeks straight, I was up all night. I cried my eyes out."

Three years later, riding at Gulfstream Park, her horse broke down and she hit the track, rolling and covering her head with her hands. Both hands were broken. At the time she was tied for leading rider at Gulfstream, but now the new injuries and the residual effects of the last one double-teamed her.

Diagnosed with post-traumatic stress disorder, Julie was in a race for her life. Suicide beckoned when the devil appeared in her nightmares. Fear hammered her like the hooves of the horse she tangled with, and depression kept her from even leaving her bed. The girl who at two years old exhibited the innate skills of horsemanship now scared the animals. "Horses felt my anxiety," she says. "They got weird."

Gradually though her daring and dashing spirit began to return. In the summer of 1996, a casual conversation with an old friend in Saratoga, New York, who happened to be a psychiatrist, opened her eyes to the value of therapy. And there were, of course, her many fans to bolster her flagging self-image.

"I was on a roller coaster of emotion. People wrote me long letters about their injuries and sent pictures of me their kids did in crayon. It was overwhelming. It made me feel, like, fed. My lifeline was racing and winning. Then suddenly, it became my friends and fans. Thinking you don't need anyone, that's not real life."

Through intense psychotherapy, medication, and the love and support of family and friends, Julie returned to racing with her old zest. She retired in 1999 and a year later, on August 7, 2000, became the first woman rider inducted into horse racing's Hall of Fame. She finished her high school degree and is studying psychology to help others with their challenges.

Julie is considered by many to be the greatest female athlete of all time. Skilled, tough, daring, determined, and honest, she also knew fear. But when pushed beyond her human limits, she learned an important lesson—to let others care.

Welcome to the winner's circle, Julie.

49

Travis Williams

Highs and lows are a part of life. Up, down—agony, ecstasy—good days, bad days—joys, sorrows. We are all familiar with the rhythms and tensions these opposites create
in our day-to-day living. In the athlete's life, winning and
losing usually determine the highs and the lows and provide the push to do one's best to win.

Every athlete I know can list the highs and lows of his
or her career and can tell you what contributed to both. I
have learned about another important quality in my career
that I have been telling you about in the stories in this
book—courage. It takes courage to deal with the despair
of defeat and not be thrown by it. It takes courage to feel
the thrill of victory and not be too inflated by it. It takes
courage to learn from both winning and losing and to become a solid person who respects one's teammates, opponents, and the game itself.

In truth, the game is only a form that teaches us to be
courageous enough to learn a simple lesson—to love, to
respond, and to share what we have with those who hurt.

When I played hockey, I didn't play so I would learn that
lesson. I played because I loved to compete, to skate, to
juke and jive, to score, to make the perfect pass, or to win

the game, the division, the playoffs, and the Stanley Cup. However, hockey taught me the importance of getting my priorities in order. I never played on a team that won the Cup. I played in the finals but we fell short. I was fortunate enough to play on the winning World Cup team in 1996. I regret that my name is not on the Stanley Cup, but I am very grateful for what I learned in my quest for it. I agree with both Grantland Rice and Vince Lombardi—how the game is played is more important than winning, but wanting to win is everything. A contradiction? I don't think so. Playing well in victory and defeat has everything to do with what we learn from both.

Travis Williams and his teammates accomplished the ultimate high of personal, professional, and team success—a Super Bowl ring. Personally he achieved success—money, reputation, family, and influence. He also experienced the agony of losing everything he had.

Travis distinguished himself in track and field at Contra Costa College in California, where he set a national junior college record for the 100-yard dash—9.3 seconds. Now that is fast! The first time Travis ever carried a football in a game was his freshman year at Contra. In his two years there he played well enough to be drafted by the Green Bay Packers in the fourth round of the 1967 draft. During his rookie year Williams returned four kickoffs for touchdowns, the first time anyone had ever done that. It was a remarkable achievement considering that Travis was so nervous during rookie camp that Coach Lombardi taped a handle on the ball so he wouldn't fumble so much. Because Travis had game-breaking speed, other defenses keyed on him. But in a playoff game against the Rams, he broke loose for two TDs from scrimmage, one a 46-yard sprint off tackle. The high point of Travis's career came on his birthday, January 14, 1968. The Packers beat the Oakland Raiders in Super Bowl II, 22–14.

Because of his speed and his ability to find daylight, Williams was nicknamed "the Roadrunner." In 1971 he was traded to the L.A. Rams, where his highlight was returning a kickoff against New Orleans 105 yards for a touchdown. The next preseason Travis blew out his knee, starting a downward spiral that he didn't reverse until the last years of his life.

He spent the next two years rehabbing his knee and trying to get back into football; however, his money ran out and the open spaces closed. He and his wife, Arie, had eight children to support.

"In 1967 I figured the money would last forever. Everybody thought I was rich and so did I," said Williams.

He started working as a security guard with the Richmond, California, school district. He sold his five cars but the accumulated debt was too much. In 1977, Arie and Travis lost their home. Travis looked back on that time with frustration: "The thing that took a lot out of me was that I could have paid for the house when I bought it. But I thought I'd play ball forever so I only put a down payment on it."

For the next few years, life spiraled out of control for the Williams family. They moved to San Francisco. An aborted dream of opening a restaurant; a job as a bouncer; an arrest for a felony battery; Arie's arrest for contributing to a death while driving drunk; and finally the children being sent to live with their grandparents—all these trials broke their spirit. Travis and Arie separated after they finished their jail time and Travis took a job in a liquor store as a security guard, a combination that eventually put him on the street living out of his car. His depression worsened and so did his drinking. He was homeless.

His life had gone from the ecstasy of a Super Bowl ring to the agonizing "security" of the "log"—a fifty-foot piece of timber on a Richmond side street, used by the homeless for shelter.

Travis finally listened to the pleas of his children and came "inside" in 1988. Their support helped him. It also enabled him to begin to make a difference in the lives of others. Homeless folk became his mission. He worked with Susan Prather, an advocate for the homeless. He invited his homeless brothers and sisters into his home when the Bay Area got cold. He never left the streets; he stayed to care. When Prather was asked about Travis and homelessness she said, "People either make it out of homelessness, or they die trying. Travis came a long way."

Travis died in February 1991 as a man who had found contentment after the highest of highs and the lowest of lows. I can't say enough about Travis and the respect I have for him. He made mistakes; he lost everything this world has to offer, but he never lost his heart. He became an advocate for the people he understood. He moved beyond the highs and lows of life. He broke into the clear on his last run because he learned lessons from both places—the courage to respond to the love of his children and to respond with love that continues to soothe the pain of his homeless friends.

50

Hank Kuehne

The mystery of family dynamics fascinates me. My personal journey in therapy has deepened my conviction that a significant part of who we are today finds its roots in the family system. Commitment to my own family is one of my highest priorities. Marybeth and I want to challenge our kids to be independent and true to themselves and to balance that freedom with values that will support them throughout life. Loving and raising kids can be the most rewarding and frightening challenge we will ever face.

Ernie and Pam Kuehne of McKinney, Texas, must understand that. They have been there. They have felt the pride of success and the tears of the pain that accompany the struggle.

Ernie's childhood in the poor, rural community of Otto, Texas, contributed to his development as a determined achiever. His self-sufficiency and take-charge attitude created in him a mix of strength and intense enthusiasm. After college and law school he found success as a trial lawyer. He quickly made senior partner and soon acquired a small bank and an oil-and-gas firm in Dallas. His intensity spilled over to his two sons and daughter. As he often said, "Ours is a family that wins and loses together. We're 100-percenters.

When we do something, the only rule we have is you have to give it your all."

Trip, Hank, and Kelli played sports as the main course of life. Pam remembers, "They played everything. Kelli was into ice skating and tennis, and the boys were involved in baseball, basketball, and football. I remember when they got their first set of real golf clubs. They used 'em as hatchets, then as swords."

Ernie's philosophy of success centered on honest feedback. His love for the children and the hard-driving fiery attitude he stoked in them stood in striking contrast to Pam's quiet, pleasant support. Ernie would observe, "Some people say, 'Never say a negative.' But I don't believe you tell someone they played good when they didn't. Hey, nothing personal. Kelli and Trip didn't mind. Hank did."

Trip sharpened his golf skills at Oklahoma State University and was a finalist in the 1994 U.S. Amateur. Kelli that same year won the Girls' Junior and went on to consecutive U.S. Women's Amateur crowns in 1995 and 1996. But the word around the community was, "They're all good, but Hank, the younger brother, he's the one to watch."

Hank was different. He carried a few more clubs in his bag but also toted extra baggage. He had to come face-to-face with dyslexia, attention deficit disorder (ADD), depression, and alcoholism. That he also possessed enormous talent only added more pressure.

As a young man, Hank struggled with his grades. The insecurity every teenager comes to know struck him particularly cruelly. He fell into depression and at the age of thirteen began to use alcohol as an escape. Even though the major contributions to his academic problems were the twin devils of dyslexia and ADD, they were not diagnosed until later. The quiet desperation would fuel a serious drinking problem.

Hank began to live with the same abandon he would use

to drive the ball over three hundred yards. Even though he was able to matriculate at Oklahoma State in 1994, Hank continued to abuse alcohol and live on the edge. Trip's recollection: "He was a complete monster."

Disaster caught up with Hank when, under the influence, he ran a stop sign and smashed into another car. Luckily, the only damage to life and limb was broken ribs in his own body and a broken leg in a passenger in the other car. Trip couldn't take any more. "I told him, 'Hank, I love you but you have to get better. Go take care of yourself.'"

Tough love can work.

"When I saw what my behavior was doing to me, my brother, and other people, I didn't want to live like that anymore," Hank says.

He checked in to Hazelden, a substance-abuse treatment center in Minnesota. He committed the next three and a half months to putting his passion into facing his alcoholism. With his family behind him, Hank was able to move out of his private hell, take ownership of his disease, and day by day, sometimes hour by hour, face the reality of a problem that had haunted him too long.

"It was so tough and he did it on his own," Kelli says. "Before he did it, he's lucky he didn't kill himself or someone else."

The support of the family that loved him came through. Kelli says, "He's awesome, he's a stud. He's worked himself out of his problems brilliantly. We've always been a big support for each other."

His victory at the 1998 U.S. Amateur capped a long and difficult road back.

"This is the second greatest victory of my life," he says. "Sobriety is definitely number one, and no matter what I do for the rest of my golfing career, nothing can change that."

SECTION 9

Senses and Sensitivity

51

Kevin Hall

Ever notice how we associate sounds with sports? We all know the groans and grunts of football, the fierce *whoosh* of hockey skates chewing up the ice, a basketball sailing through the net.

Golf has its own unique set of sounds. The sweet thunk of a solid drive. That distinctive plink when the ball drops into the cup after a perfect putt.

Kevin Hall can make those sounds pretty well, enough to be named the 1999 Junior Golfer of the Year by the Minority Golf Foundation. He can make those sounds but he cannot hear them. Kevin Hall is eighteen; he lost his hearing at the age of two.

Neither Kevin nor his parents, Percy and Jackie, ever let his deafness come between him and achievement. Kevin was first academically in his class at St. Rita in Evendale, Ohio, a suburb of Cincinnati, and earned a scholarship (part academic, part athletic) to Ohio State University.

"You have to find the positive in what happens and that's what Kevin has done," says his mother, who works for Ryder Transportation Services. "He has not let the loss of hearing dampen his spirits or kill his love of life."

Kevin welcomes the platform his unusual combination

of skills and traits affords him. He likes the idea of inspiring others to fight the good fight against whatever it might be that could hold them back.

"I see many African-Americans with no hope and no goals," he says. "I feel if they see a person of their race succeed, they will feel they can do it too."

Kevin's struggle began when he was an infant. He spent a month in the hospital, burning up with a 103-degree temperature for two weeks after contracting H-flu meningitis. Once the fever broke, his parents quickly noticed a change in their only child.

"We'd pop a balloon behind him or call his name and he wasn't responding," Jackie says. "We knew almost immediately he'd lost his hearing."

Percy was the first to learn sign language, and he and Jackie quickly read up on deafness and its consequences. They labeled all the objects in the house to help Kevin learn that these things had names and tried to reach him through finger spelling. By the time he was three he knew his phone number and his address.

"The more we taught him, the more he wanted to know," Jackie says. "He took off and never looked back."

Kevin began playing golf when he was nine and captained the golf team at Winton Woods High in Forest Park, Ohio (St. Rita's had no golf team, so Kevin was allowed to play elsewhere). As a senior, he won the individual section and division championships and finished fourth in the Division I state tournament.

One thing Kevin knows he must deal with is media pressure. When he played in the U.S. Junior Amateur in 1999, he drew crowds of reporters. He told his mother he wished he wouldn't get so much attention and that he just wanted to be "normal." Here's what Jackie told him: "How many black kids do you see playing golf at the level you are? How many deaf black kids? Let's make a decision. Do you want to quit or play?"

Kevin wants to play, no question. He met Tiger Woods at a clinic and got some tips on putting and adding more length to his drives. He says his goal is to one day defeat Tiger in a match.

Imagine that happening, and a crowd cheering, and Kevin taking all of it in. Not hearing anything, of course, but reveling in it anyway, soaking it in with his other senses.

"I don't need to be able to hear those sounds to fully enjoy golf," he says. "I use my eyes like hearing people use their ears. That's enough for me. Feeling the club hit the ball and feeling the ground after the ball falls in the cup is wonderful and satisfying."

52

Marla Runyan

She's going to be mad at me. She hates for this story to be told this way. She can't stand it when people get the idea that she exceeded the perceived limits placed on her rather than fulfilled her potential.

"If I break a national record," she says, "maybe they will stop writing about my eyes. It's a matter of commitment. Some people have a bad attitude, and that's their disability."

Marla Runyan is thirty-one and legally blind. Yet in 1999, running the 1500 meters, she won gold at the Pan Am Games, finished fourth at the USA Track & Field Outdoor Championships, and tenth at the World Championships in Seville, Spain.

Sorry, Marla, but here we go with another list of all the things you can't do: see the finish line, read a stopwatch, watch a tape of your races without sitting with your face practically against the TV screen.

And she is right to be angry that the focus always seems to be on the things she can't do, when she has done so much.

Her medical condition is called Stargardt's disease. It's a progressive degeneration of the retina that has left her with a gaping hole in the middle of her visual field. She has 20-

300 vision in one eye, 20-400 in the other. But in 2000 she won the USA Track & Field Indoor Championships at 3000 meters, leading wire to wire to win in 9:01.29.

"Please," she asks, "think of me as an athlete, not a legally blind athlete." And what an athletic life she has had.

As a nine-year-old in Camarillo, California, her vision began to go. At fourteen she couldn't see well enough to follow a soccer ball, so she began to run track and compete in field events, setting a school record with a high jump of 5 feet 7 inches.

At San Diego State she broadened her focus to seven events—the heptathlon. When she lost the ability to see the hurdles, she counted the steps from the start to the first one and then on to the next, running almost by memory.

With the help of her mother, Valerie, she also succeeded in academics. She wore a magnifying device attached to her glasses so she could read large-print books, and her mother would help by writing out, in large type, the assigned reading material from her classes. She graduated cum laude from San Diego State in 1991 and then earned a master's degree in education of the handicapped.

"The biggest thing her mother and I did was not to set up any artificial barriers for Marla," says her father, Gary. "We let her find her own barriers. Some she found painfully. But she also found things she could do."

Yes, like waterskiing and scuba diving. She even got a California driver's license. And she also made the 2000 U.S. Olympic team, placing eighth in the 1500 meters in Sydney.

So often we set our goals based on what we see. Think about Marla Runyan. Her goals exist in a world largely unseen. She can barely make out the shape of the other competitors on the track, and so she must continually refine the runner's intuition that is so critical to having a sense of where she and the others are in the race.

Don't be too mad at me, Marla. I know you get tired of

being held up as an example of how people can persevere and overcome, and I know I'm doing it to you again. But I'm impressed that someone who cannot see the tape at the end of the race can be dedicated enough to be the first through that unseen barrier.

Marla Runyan can barely see. But she never took her eyes off the prize.

53

Jamel Bradley

The ball swished through the net but Jamel Bradley didn't hear it.

The *thump-thump-thump* of his basketball on the hard blacktop laid down an impressive rhythm that Jamel could feel. But he couldn't hear it.

It is no surprise to me that Jamel Bradley has such a powerful, positive influence on young hearing-impaired kids. His role as a smooth shooting guard on the University of South Carolina basketball team plays a part, but the more critical factor is that he too is hearing impaired.

When Jamel was eighteen months old, he lost his ability to hear well. Running a 103-degree temperature for three days did him in. He grew up in a mostly silent world, feeling different and ashamed. Like most kids, he desperately wanted to fit in, especially as he grew older, but his hearing loss caused him to gradually withdraw.

"It was difficult. I built a wall around myself. I felt nobody wanted to talk to me when they saw my hearing aids. I was a loner. It took a while before I was able to reach out and touch people."

At six foot two, 160 pounds, Jamel lacks a physically imposing presence, but his forte is not size. It's his jump shot.

Playing sports helped Jamel begin to move out of his quiet, solitary space.

He started playing basketball on a local playground in Beckley, West Virginia. Sharon Bradley, Jamel's mom, says that her son's love of basketball shifted into high gear when he was in elementary school. He'd come home, do his homework, then go to the YMCA to play ball. He was at the Y every chance he had. He kept improving and kept working, and soon his brother and his friends started inviting him to play in their games.

"Things started clicking. They were in junior high school and a couple years older than me. They told me to stay in the corner. They'd pass the ball to me and I'd shoot," Jamel says.

He practiced and played every chance he got, and when he started high school he stepped into a leadership role, helping Woodrow Wilson High School in Beckley to back-to-back class AAA titles his final two seasons. His senior year he set the West Virginia high school record for free throw accuracy, connecting on 95 of 100 from the line. His coach, David Barkesdale, speaks highly of his former pupil.

"He never complained. I saw him take charges that would send a hearing aid flying one way and the other going in an opposite direction. He never used it as a crutch. He was an inspiration to all of us."

When Jamel got to the University of South Carolina, he was fitted with digital, programmable, omnidirectional hearing aids that help him hear sounds from every direction. These aids have improved his hearing by 85 percent. He can hear his coach and his teammates and a whole lot more.

He now enjoys listening to rhythm-and-blues tunes, birds chirping, and traffic signals buzzing. At a rock concert a while back he complained the music was too loud—a nice problem for a young guy who communicated with his coach through hand signals. Those hand signals his coach used in high school are no longer necessary. Now his coach yelling at him sounds like sweet music.

In turn, the Southeastern Conference is now "hearing" from Bradley. In his sophomore year, Jamel was an occasional starter and led the team in scoring in four games. At one point near the end of the 1999–2000 season, he had connected on 36 of 84 three-point attempts (42.9 percent) and was 14 of 17 (82.4 percent) from the free throw line.

Today, Jamel Bradley inspires the hearing impaired— young and old. His success with the Gamecocks resonates with young kids throughout the country, and his words encourage them to manage their handicap differently than he did when he was their age. Jamel speaks frequently to groups of the hearing impaired in and around Columbia, South Carolina. He talks to struggling individual kids as well. He reached out to one young person in Florence, South Carolina, who was having trouble relating to classmates and teammates.

Jamel's simple message: "Always wear your hearing aid." He understands the struggle. He didn't wear his because he desperately wanted to fit in.

"I let them know I'm in the same shoes they are," he says. "They don't wear hearing aids because they think people won't talk to them. I tell them to keep their hearing aids and listen to what everyone says."

Jamel Bradley earned a place on the United States Deaf Olympic Team, which competed in Rome in 1999. With his college career moving into his junior and senior years, who knows what he will achieve on the hardwood? What I do know is that, athletic success aside, he is already a hero to hearing-impaired kids and adults.

One of Jamel's young friends, Christopher Thompson, put it this way: "It is great to know there is someone out there that's the same as you."

54

Donnell Finnaman

Despite asthma and nagging sore knees, Donnell Finnaman didn't miss a practice in four years. Playing both offensive and defensive tackle in Class 1A North Carolina High School Athletic Association men's varsity competition for four years spoke of a passion to succeed and excel.

Watching the five-foot-six, 140-pound tackle pull out on a bootleg and clear the way for the quarterback run left no reason to doubt Coach Leonard Baker's boasts of Donnell's unusual talent. As one well-beaten opponent put it, "Finnaman is the best I've ever faced."

It was not an easy thing to acknowledge. Donnell is a girl and she is deaf.

When she was born in Egg Harbor, New Jersey, she weighed two pounds. Her twin brother, Donovan, appeared twenty minutes later and tipped the scales at three pounds. Both little ones needed special care because of their premature arrival. Donovan had more difficulty because of respiratory troubles. At two, Donnell also developed complications in her hearing.

Her ears functioned normally, but the signals to the brain never arrived. She was diagnosed with neural nerve deafness. Doctors recommended she attend a special school away from home, in Trenton, New Jersey.

The separation from the family was difficult for her mother, Marchelle, and they soon moved to Fayetteville, North Carolina, and enrolled Donnell in the East North Carolina School for the Deaf (ENCSD) when she was in the third grade. "She was able to have a regular life, do the things that other children do, be a leader," her mother says.

Donnell grew up with the label of tomboy. She loved football and perfected her tackling by taking on her twin brother in the backyard. After a few years she signed up for intramurals at ENCSD. By the eighth grade she had started talking to Baker about playing varsity football. He had no misgivings about her becoming part of the team.

"I knew that Donnell was serious, and that she was a talented athlete," he recalls. The coach talked with Marchelle, checked with the state association to make sure there were no restrictions, and ran it past the rest of the squad, gaining unanimous approval.

"I asked her if she was sure," says Marchelle. "I was afraid but proud that my daughter never really heard the word *can't.*"

Donnell remembers the beginning challenge: "I had to show that I was physical and that I was not afraid to play with the boys and that I was tough."

On the first day of practice, the freshman Donnell was behind the tackling dummy. A senior charged it, plowed his shoulder in, and knocked her down. She jumped up and signed (by pointing to her wrist) the phrase "one more time." He tried again and she stood him up straight.

Playing football is not just a novelty or a publicity stunt for her. She was ranked as ENCSD's top offensive lineman at the end of her junior season. "I have personal pride," she signs, "but my greatest pride is playing a team sport. I want any focus on me to shift to the team."

When football is over for the season, Finnaman will concentrate on basketball. She has played center for the Fighting Hornets for three years. In the spring, she will be a favorite to win the state Class 1A shot put title. She has earned this label by finishing among the top ten in the shot in the NCHSAA 1A Track championships for the past three years.

They love Donnell at ENCSD. Fans wave the foam rubber hands to spell the letters I-L-Y or "I Love You." Donnell wants to be remembered "as a leader, a good athlete, and as a football player too." She has single-handedly introduced the word "linewoman" to the world of varsity football.

"Some people say I'm special," she says, "but I don't see myself that way."

I do, Donnell. You are a very special Companion in Courage. Few could accomplish what you have. Fewer still would tackle it.

SECTION 10

From the Heart

55

Brian Grant

Professional athletes do a lot of good in their communities, and I wish that they got more publicity for their efforts. The bad stuff always gets in the newspapers or on TV, but the hours spent helping others just don't seem to make a good story.

At least that's the way the media seems to look at it. I see it, quite naturally, from the athlete's side. And while I think players should be acknowledged for their positive contributions, I know that's not their motivation. They get plenty of cheers and applause elsewhere.

They do it to do good. The giving of their time and compassion comes back tenfold in emotional payoffs. And while I heartily support all the wonderful programs athletes conceive and execute, I'm most thrilled and moved when athletes dedicate themselves to children. That's how I learned about Brian Grant and why I'm proud to include him as a Companion in Courage.

Dash Thomas, a twelve-year-old boy suffering from cancer, first introduced me to Brian. During the NBA lockout in 1998 I heard Dash say that Brian, a forward for the Portland Trail Blazers, was his best friend. Because so many of the children that I met at Buffalo General's cancer ward numbered among my best friends, I decided I needed to know more about Brian Grant.

During the lockout Brian started driving to Sublimity, Oregon, a one-hour ride from Portland, to visit Dash, who had been diagnosed with brain cancer. Dash, a young white kid, and Brian, a black NBA power forward who wore dreadlocks, forged a firm friendship. They became each other's heroes.

When the lockout ended, Brian wanted to get Dash to a game. Unfortunately, that never happened. His young friend died in February. Brian dedicated his season to Dash Thomas.

The NBA lockout will be remembered as a labor dispute, a fight between millionaire players and billionaire owners. Brian Grant got something entirely different from it. "Because of the lockout, Dash died before he could come to a game. On the other hand, without the lockout, I wouldn't have had as much time to get to know him," he said. "There was something about the way he carried himself. He wasn't like a twelve-year-old kid. It was like he was older. His courage—everything about him—was amazing. He was an inspiration. My relationship with Dash changed my life."

During the playoffs, Grant battled the best power forward in the league, Karl Malone, to a standoff. During their epic struggle one of Malone's famous elbows caught Brian in the right eye, opening a gash that took six stitches to close. It also opened a window into his psyche.

While many of Brian's fellow NBA players played AAU (Amateur Athletic Union) basketball and in the much-touted summer camps before being drafted, Brian was cutting tobacco and baling hay back in Georgetown, Ohio. He watched his dad and uncles weld boxcars—hard, nasty, physical labor. He saw them, with no first-aid kits available and no time to waste, slice potatoes in half and put them on their cuts to ease the pain from their burns. One night

Grant's father came home with a bandage over his eye. He had been hit by a piece of hot metal.

So a six-stitch gash? What should that mean next to the struggles of Brian's father, his uncles, and a frail twelve-year-old named Dash, hospitalized in Sublimity, Oregon? Brian's attitude? "Stitch it up and let's play!"

Brian continues to excel in the NBA, though he now plays with the Miami Heat, but he also stands out in his work with children.

Brian has many young friends and a growing list of community leaders who respect him. His future holds so much promise. But he is never, ever far from his past, never really removed from family in Georgetown, Ohio, or separated from the memory of a boy named Dash.

56

Jeannette Jay

Every day for years I have strapped my kids into car seats for their safety. Now I find out that Mighty Pete Sawicki would have his fourteen-year-old daughter do handstands on the back of his motorcycle while riding in parades. Is that wild or what?

For Pete's little girl Jeannette, it was just one more experience that reinforced her need for constant activity and attention. In fact, if she were in the same school today in the Genesee-Fillmore neighborhood of Buffalo, the powers that be would have slapped that "attention deficit disorder" label on her. "I was this hyperactive kid who couldn't sit still," she recalls. "I was doing cartwheels in the classrooms, headstands on roofs."

Her sister Christelle, now Sister Christelle and principal of Blessed Sacrament School in Buffalo, puts her memories of Jeannette to work in a positive fashion. "I see kids like that now and see potential, and I always share with kids her story because I feel education doesn't always prepare us for what God wants us to do in life," she says.

Jeannette was a handful, fearless and spirited. She could be dramatic when she needed the spotlight. She recalls drinking a bottle of ink to get the attention of her fourth-grade friends because they were ignoring her cartwheels. She could also test the limits of those who loved her—she simply could not sit still. Eventually the nuns asked that Jeannette leave Transfiguration School because of how difficult she was to handle.

No telling of her story is complete without the now-famous incident in the German Day parade. She was fourteen and ready to perform her motorcycle stunt with Mighty Pete.

"He used to signal me to kick up on the back of the bike, and I'd do a handstand; my foot would rest on his shoulder," she says. "I wasn't paying attention and . . . he pulled away. I went to kick to the handstand and I went flat on my face. I was bleeding all over the place. He wanted me to be great. So he said, 'Get back on that bike. I don't care if you are bleeding.' Everyone in the audience was clapping. 'Yeah, little girl.' I'm fourteen years old, blood all over the place, and I got up on that bike, and it made me tough, and my dad made me who I am today."

After attending business school and working in a local health club, Jeannette left Buffalo to travel with "The Great Unis," a strongman show in which she performed her gymnastics. Her athletic abilities helped her learn to be an accomplished tightwire performer and trapeze artist. She appeared on the *Ed Sullivan Show* and in the Ringling Bros. circus. She settled in Pittsburgh, where she began to follow her dream to coach and teach gymnastics to others.

Eventually she opened three schools and was nominated as the small businesswoman of the year. She never lost her flair. She celebrated her forty-eighth birthday by doing a handstand on top of a limousine at the Pittsburgh Sheraton.

Jeannette's gymnastic curriculum was unique. She created routines that involved an obstacle course, as opposed to the traditional practice regimen. The flexibility this lent the program only enhanced it. Each individual could approach the course at different speeds and levels based on a wide range of abilities. The excitement for Jeannette came from creating a new sport that worked with and for highly skilled athletes as well as the physically challenged.

"Some people brought a Down's syndrome kid with them to try the program, and they were ecstatic," she says. "The child loved the program. It's kind of hard work, but it's fun hard work. There are no weights involved in this, yet they will strengthen their body by doing the obstacle course repetitively. That's the key."

Jeannette knew a little something about obstacle courses. Her life became one in 1993 when she suffered severe injuries in a head-on car crash. She went through eleven surgeries, including dental surgery for a broken jaw and damaged teeth, and had a metal rod inserted in her broken leg. Her new "obstacle course" included two weeks in the hospital, four months in bed, and eight months in a wheelchair. She had to liquidate her business and eventually sold all three schools. But as her father had taught her, it was "time to get back up on the bike."

Unwilling as she was to yield to the damage or the pain, Jeannette's recovery virtually obscures the fact that she was ever injured. "My hope is still to walk on my hands. I miss demonstrating to the kids. I used to demonstrate everything. Now when I do it, the mind wants to but the body suffers the next day," she says.

As if the accident wasn't enough, her plans for a new, $1.5-million school in Pittsburgh, an anniversary party to celebrate twenty-five years of teaching and a fiftieth birthday all went up in smoke—literally. Jeannette lost her house in a fire.

"All I could think about was, maybe I better go home," she says. "I was standing in front of a mirror a week after the fire, and I called my sister and I said, 'You know, Sister Christelle, maybe I better come home.' " Home she is.

Jeannette Jay is building another school in Buffalo, teaching kids at all levels of need and harboring a dream to host the first national Junior Fitness Challenge in Buffalo in 2001.

"I have a focus and a passion on this, and that's what keeps me going every day," she says. "I can't even sleep anymore from the excitement. I get up at three or four in the morning and my brain's going a mile a minute."

It's probably just trying to keep up with her body.

Jerry Sandusky

Jerry Sandusky helps people. Whether they are overcoming the disadvantages of a tough background or another team's offensive schemes, Sandusky pours himself into giving them an edge.

The seeds for Sandusky's work were planted in Washington, Pennsylvania, where he lived with his parents, Art and Evie. Their small apartment was surrounded by a recreational center that his parents directed. Jerry was a part of whatever game was on. He learned to compete. He learned to love and respect people. He learned to laugh and to give his all.

When Sandusky enrolled at Penn State in the early sixties, he couldn't begin to guess that he'd call State College home for many years to come. He played defensive end for the Nittany Lions, got his degree, and stuck around as a graduate assistant. After brief coaching stints at Juniata College and Boston University in 1969, he was hired as an assistant coach at his alma mater. In 1977 he became defensive coordinator—the mastermind behind the awesome Penn State defenses that helped lead the Nittany Lions to two national championships.

Jerry retired after the 1999 season, logging thirty-two

years as an assistant and twenty-three years as defensive coordinator. He made his name developing twelve first-team All-America linebackers. His book, *Developing Linebackers the Penn State Way*, chronicles his approach and attention to every detail.

Before Sandusky became the defensive coordinator at Penn State, he was offered the head coaching job at Marshall University. He accepted and then declined. That sudden turnaround defines the compassion and courage of Jerry Sandusky more than all his achievements as a coach.

After negotiating a contract agreement with Marshall and agreeing to it, Jerry came downstairs to announce the news to his family. The first child to greet him was a young foster kid he and his wife, Dottie, were caring for. The youngster ran up to Jerry and asked him if they could go outside and play ball. He looked out the window and the other kids were outside playing in the snow. In that moment, Sandusky made another decision. He knew he couldn't go to Marshall and leave these kids.

He wanted to be a head coach. But more than that, he wanted to give these needy children what he knew they needed—attention, direction, and love.

Prior to the Marshall decision, Jerry and Dottie had been developing a group foster home. Those plans grew into the "Second Mile," a nonprofit charitable foundation for disadvantaged youth. Today the program has twenty full-time employees and services a network of volunteers, fundraisers, and school and community programs that help give thousands of kids a chance to live productive lives.

As the Sanduskys' involvement grew, so did their family—Jerry and Dottie adopted six children, Ray, E. J., Kara, Jeff, Matt, and Jon. Matt, twenty-one, speaks for all the Sandusky kids: "My life changed when I came here. There were rules, there was discipline, there was caring. Dad put me on a workout program. He gave me someone to talk to, a father figure I never had. I have no idea where I'd be without Mom and him. I don't even want to think about it. And they've helped so many kids besides me."

In many ways, what Dottie and Jerry do harks back to Art and Evie's recreation program in Washington, Pennsylvania. E. J. describes his dad as "a frustrated playground director." He fondly remembers the kickball games his father organized in the family backyard: "Dad would get every single kid involved. We had the largest kickball games, with forty kids."

Competition and passion made Jerry go. At the summer football camp, the feature was not just football. It was the entertainment competition between the "Great Pretenders"—fellow Penn State coaches Joe Sarra, Bill Kenney, and Sandusky—and Spider, also known as assistant equipment manager Brad Caldwell. Spider always won. Sandusky finally outdid Spider by going to the great lengths of having him arrested by the campus police. When he gave his farewell address at the Penn State Quarterback Club dinner, Jerry reviewed his memorable years as a coach but also announced with great joy that Spider had finally lost.

Whether it's a backyard kickball game or an important bowl game, the common ingredients are commitment and passion. All-America linebacker LaVar Arrington recalls an incident that took place in Miami during Penn State's game against the Hurricanes on September 18, 1999. Arrington had gotten carried away by the frenzy of the game and was exchanging taunts with the crowd. Sandusky spotted him and charged toward him. He tripped over a wire, scattering equipment and landing on his face, all the while screaming, "Don't do that!" When Arrington turned to see what all the noise was about, he saw his coach sprawled on the sidelines, yelling at him. He couldn't help himself. He laughed.

"He gets caught up in the moment sometimes," Arrington said.

On November 13, 1999, Jerry Sandusky ran out onto the Beaver Stadium field for the last time as a Penn State football coach. He received a standing ovation and was greeted by his sons Jon, a defensive back, and Matt, a team manager. They hugged one another, and thousands of kids felt that embrace as they watched in the stands and on TV. With tears in his eyes, Jerry told his sons to get lost because he had a game to coach, and then he headed for the sidelines.

What will he do now? He will continue to help run the Second Mile program, do volunteer work with the athletic department's Life Skills and Outreach programs, coach at football camps, write another book, and—who knows?—maybe even coach somewhere again.

LaVar is right. Jerry Sandusky does get caught up in the moment. Thank God he does. It doesn't matter whether he's trying to outperform Spider at a summer football camp, beat back the poverty and injustice that affect young kids' lives, defend his goal line against the best teams in America, or organize backyard kickball games, Jerry gives his all. He brings passion, vision, and commitment to his every effort.

Thanks to Jerry Sandusky, Happy Valley and a whole lot of people have been a little bit happier for a long, long time.

58

Peter Westbrook

In a fifth-floor studio on West 25th Street in Manhattan, kids learn how to fight. No, it's not what you think. This place doesn't have a boxing ring, a wrestling mat, or martial arts instructors. It's a club for fencers run by Peter Westbrook, the bronze medalist in fencing at the 1984 Los Angeles Olympic Games. Peter, who left his job with IBM and the *New York Times* to start a fencing program for kids in upstate New York, knows that life on the streets is very much about protecting yourself from danger.

He grew up in the Hayes Homes Housing Project in Newark, New Jersey, and, like many young kids, ran with the "fast" crowd in his neighborhood.

"I was very slick. I used to hang out with some real fast people," he says.

Mariko, Westbrook's mother, grew concerned about the direction of her son's life, so she took a job at a nearby rectory so Peter could attend Essex Catholic, a private high school. Once at Essex, Peter joined the fencing team, which became the first step toward turning around not only his own life but those of many others.

The transformation took time.

"I didn't change right away. But fencing gave me an outlet for my aggression," he says. "The first time I had that sword in my hand, I realized this is a fighting sport. God knows I did my share of fighting. But over time, as I watched my friends either go to jail or die, I realized I didn't want to take my hurt out on other people anymore."

Peter continued to excel as a fencer, a relief and a source of pride for his mother, since Samurai warriors were a part of her Japanese heritage. He won a scholarship to New York University and achieved Olympic stardom. A combination of successful sales skills and fencing expertise led him to establish the Peter Westbrook Foundation with Mika'il Sankofa, the only four-time NCAA champion and an Olympic teammate. His plan was simple: Expose kids from different cultures to fencing and to one another; provide academic help; and give them a constructive outlet for their emotions. He began the program with $10,000 and seven students.

The Westbrook Foundation now has sponsors and is able to charge $20 a year or whatever each kid can afford. Peter, who is of African-American and Japanese descent, runs a weekly class for eighty to one hundred kids and an after-school program for his top thirty students. When the Olympic fencing team arrived in Sydney for the 2000 Games, three of the six fencers were products of Westbrook's program.

In addition to making a difference in hundreds of kids' lives, Peter's work has produced Keeth Smart, a two-time NCAA saber champion, and Akhi Spencer-El, the first American to be ranked as the world's Number 1 in sabre.

The story of Harvey Miller, one of Westbrook's students, is an example of what happens at the club. Two years ago, Harvey fit the profile of a kid going nowhere. He was flunking out of school and hanging out on the streets of Queens. He hadn't passed a course at school in two years. When Miller's mother heard of Westbrook's program, she gave him an ultimatum: "It's either fencing or boot camp." Harvey chose fencing.

Peter went with the young man to school to talk to the counselors. Harvey agreed to attend daily and to take night classes to make up the courses he had flunked. In the second term of the 1999 school year, Harvey earned a place on the honor roll.

"In fencing I was a natural. I fenced well and that inspired me to do well in other areas of my life," Harvey says.

Harvey Miller finished third in saber at the North American Cup in South Bend, Indiana, in early 2000 and competed in the Junior Olympics in Sacramento.

"I have no doubt. Fencing and Peter saved my life," he says.

On the floor at the club, Coach Sankofa barks out the commands and the fencers move in unison, "Advance. Retreat. Lunge. En garde."

The class—short kids, tall kids, black, white, skinny and plump kids—goes through its fencing routines. Peter Westbrook watches with pride as his pupils learn lessons that give them a fighting chance at the club, in competition, and on the streets where they live.

"I just knew fencing would help these kids, just as it helped me," Westbrook says. "Some of them have a natural fighting spirit. Give them some technical training, encourage a sense of self-discipline, convince them to give back to others, and God will take care of the rest."

In a world full of violence and weapons, what a wonderful thing to see Peter Westbrook not taking, but giving, at the point of a sword.

59

Steve Beuerlein

When they played high school football together, Jeff Sherer protected Steve Beuerlein.

Now it's Steve's turn to look out for his friend.

Sherer played offensive tackle for Servite High in Anaheim, California. His buddy, the quarterback, went on to fame at the University of Notre Dame and then into the NFL, where he's now the Carolina Panthers' Pro Bowl passer.

Beuerlein makes a good living as an NFL player, using his brains and his body. Sherer, thirty-four, can hardly move at all. Sherer suffers from Lou Gehrig's disease—otherwise known as amyotrophic lateral sclerosis. This terrible and debilitating disorder of the nervous system progressively weakens its victims and ultimately kills them, usually within two to five years of diagnosis. Gehrig, the New York Yankees first baseman, died when he was thirty-eight. ALS also claimed pitcher Jim "Catfish" Hunter in 1999.

Sherer learned he had the disease in 1998. From then on, Beuerlein and thirteen others who played with them at Servite joined to support their friend in any way they could—emotionally and financially. They've helped provide for the family, paid medical bills, and staged an annual golf tournament to raise even more money for the Sherers. When Steve went to Hawaii for the Pro Bowl, his first in his thirteen-year career, he brought Jeff and his wife, Marya.

Last May, at the invitation of Pennsylvania senator Arlen Specter, Beuerlein testified before a U.S. Senate subcommittee to raise awareness about ALS. He was more than glad to do it. With him were Jeff and Marya, to bring home dramatically what ALS does to those who suffer from it and also how it afflicts their loved ones. Jeff and Marya have three children, the youngest just five months old at the time of Steve's visit to the Senate and the oldest a mere four years. Steve did the talking, using his status as a professional football player to touch hearts.

He talked about Jeff and the progressive weakening ALS inflicted on his old teammate. "This once-tremendous athlete no longer has the use of his arms or legs. His five-month-old son, he has never been able to pick up and hold and say that he loves him. Imagine the pain and frustration that goes with that."

No stranger to speaking to large groups, Steve Beuerlein had much more to talk about than how the Panthers might do next season. His stature brought with it an obligation he happily met.

"It's an example of the opportunity we have as professional athletes," he says. "People tend to pay a little more attention to you. I've always looked at it as one of my responsibilities, to stand up for the things you believe in and to try and make a difference in a positive way if you can."

Good point. There is so much competition for funding that a spokesman with star power can really make a difference. It's a shame that decisions might be made based on that, but it's also a reality.

"In Washington, we have what we call 'disease wars' going on right now," says Steve Gibson of the ALS Association. "Without bringing high-profile people in to tell the story, you really aren't able to put a face on the horrors of a disease like ALS."

Horrors is the right word. Jeff Sherer spends most of his days in a wheelchair and cannot move his arms or legs. A machine aids his breathing at night. Speech doesn't come easy, yet his mind remains active. He can form thoughts; ALS won't let him express them. Imagine his anguish when he wants to tell his children he loves them or to thank his wife for her kind and loving attention.

"Jeff is always wondering why he is the one who has this, like a lot of people would in his situation," Marya says. "It's one of those things that makes you realize there is a reason for everything and a purpose. You feel like what you're going through isn't for nothing."

Steve Beuerlein can't cure his friend. But he can help and he did help and he will continue to do so, using his public standing to advance a cause.

"There are very few times in your life when you really have a chance, an individual chance, to do one thing that can make a big difference and really have a significant impact. This might have been a once-in-a-lifetime opportunity for me."

60

Esther Kim

We have talked about courage in its many forms throughout the many stories in this book. We've looked at the private wars people fought against their inner demons, their
struggles with disease, loss of limbs, loss of life. I know I'm
a better person for the knowledge I've gained. The grace
and dignity we've witnessed is astounding and touching.

But there's another aspect of courage—the will to do the
right thing, even at great personal expense. This is no small
mountain to scale. If doing the right thing were easy, everyone would do it. Unfortunately, we don't live in that world.

Now ask yourself this: What would you do for your friend?
What sacrifice would you make for a person you love and
respect—even if it meant giving up your own dream? Let
me tell you about Esther Kim and her willingness to part
with her own goals for the sake of her friend.

We'll go back to May 2000, at the U.S. Olympic tae-
kwondo trials. Competing in the flyweight division, and
ranked Number 1 in the world, is eighteen-year-old Kay
Poe. Olympic observers figure she's a sure thing for a gold
medal in Australia. But, in her semifinal victory, she dislo-
cates her left kneecap.

She is clearly in no condition to compete in the final,

and her opponent, Esther Kim, knows it. Esther, twenty, and Kay have been friends and training partners for years.

Understand this: In order for Esther to make the team, she would have to defeat Kay. She also knew that, with both of them healthy, she probably would not win. In her heart, Esther knew Kay was the better of the two.

Now how many of us would have felt pity for our pal but, with an Olympic berth on the line, gone ahead and kicked their butt? Yeah, a lot of people. Hey, breaks of the game, that sort of stuff, right? We're a society that judges on wins and losses. We say things like, "All's fair in love and war" and "To the victor go the spoils" and "It ain't cheatin' if you don't get caught."

But not Esther. Esther wanted to win in a sportsmanlike way or not at all. She needed to defeat the reigning top-ranked fighter in her division in hand-to-hand combat, with the better person winning. This, of course, could not be. And so she decided to forfeit the match, sending Kay to the Olympics.

"It would have been unfair to fight someone with one leg," Esther said.

I still find myself saying "Wow!" when I tell this story. You work at a sport your entire life and it gets added to the Olympics just as your career is peaking and you forfeit the key match out of a sense of fair play and respect for a friend. Let me say it again—Wow!

Know what? This story gets better. Esther still gets to go to Australia.

Moved by her gesture, IOC president Juan Antonio Samaranch offered to pay for Esther and her father, who coaches both women, to go to Sydney to see Kay Poe compete. He called from an IOC meeting in Rio de Janeiro to express his thanks for her living the Olympic ideal.

The two Houston natives, friends for thirteen years, embraced and bowed after the match that never was. Esther told Kay, "We won." Her father puts it this way: "I hope that this act that Esther took [sends] a message to all athletes how important it is to make sacrifices."

As Esther's decision was announced at the trials, she and her father escorted the limping Kay to the mat. The crowd cheered and applauded. Who had ever seen anything like this? Yes, some tears were shed. It doesn't matter that Kay lost her first and only Olympic match in Sydney.

"A few years from now, I'll look back on this," Esther says. "I will smile a lot and feel proud."

Esther, there is no point in waiting and no time like the present. You have touched us in a way that no victory, no gold medal, no accolade or award, ever could.

Conclusion

We all have a story—where we began, what happens while we're here, how we manage, what we learn, and how we continue. Reading the stories of others gives us a chance to walk in their shoes, to experience their challenges and their triumphs.

It wasn't until I met Robert, Erik, Angela, Jessica, Paul, Teresa, and all of the other kids at Buffalo's Children's Hospital and Roswell Park that I began to appreciate the power of another person's story. Being with those kids—knowing their smiles, their pain, and their courage—changed my life.

They taught me about life and death. They taught me the meaning of toughness, courage, and love. These children and their stories leave me with two simple realities: Things happen to us and we have to respond. We don't always have much control over what happens to us, but we do have a choice in how we respond.

We can feel as if we are just victims of our misfortune. Or we can tap into that deep, inner place within us and find a way to make our way through the challenge, be it illness, injury, or the death of a friend or loved one.

Inner place? I had only heard of such an idea. Then I came face-to-face with my own hurt. When I thought I was

losing my mind and when darkness haunted me, I came
to know desperation. I was in the fight of my life. I needed
help. I'm forever grateful I got it.

This inner place is peaceful, and it is always there. It does
not go away when good or bad things happen to us. I didn't
personally experience this place until I was pushed beyond
my own human limits and I saw children and their families pushed beyond theirs.

The inner place is a place of love and strength. Love is
really who we are. What happens to us doesn't change that.
Love is a powerful form of energy that strengthens and
comforts us when we tap it. How do we find it? Here's what
I have learned so far.

When I couldn't cope, I was forced to reach out. I learned
to let people help me. When my friend John Brown died,
when asthma almost grounded my athletic career, when I
fell through the ice and almost drowned, somehow I survived and moved on. Up until my athletic injuries, that's
how life worked for me. I got help along the way, went to
church, and was confident and secure I could get through
anything. My injuries taught me the importance of letting
others help. The more love is given and received, the
stronger it gets.

I learned to back up and look at the big picture. I realized I learn from whatever happens—good or bad. Getting
help, telling my story, learning from it, listening, and seeing the big picture helped me discover that giving to others leads me to that inner place of love.

In many ways, I lived the kind of life that others dream
of. But professional athletes are just people, facing the very
real issues that confront everyone. I'm fortunate. My own
story had a happy ending. Despite several severe injuries,
my hockey career continued and flourished. For that I owe
a debt to several doctors, especially James Kelly, and other
fine men in hockey like my coach in Buffalo, Ted Nolan.

Sure, I worked hard to get back each time, but I could not have done it without their help. When I took the ice in what would be my last season, playing for the New York Rangers, I remember feeling so fortunate that I could still play the game and enjoy it. If everything I endured taught me only one thing, it's that you can never take anything for granted. You must live in each moment and cherish it, because it will soon be gone. Whether it's loving your family or your work (and ideally it would be both), do it *NOW!* Tomorrow holds no assurances.

I don't kid myself. I'm not telling you life is without its risks, its losses, its fear and pain. I *am* telling you to revel in life's glories. I know that you can prevail over doubt, despair, and illness. The truth is we are resilient. Our strength lies within, just waiting to be tapped, often obscured by fear and ignorance.

We're not in this alone. Often that is a hard idea to accept. We think we need to work all of this out by ourselves, but we're mistaken in trying to fly solo. Reaching out can be so hard. But as we fight to find that inner place, we will learn to lean on family and friends for strength and comfort. They will give it freely, out of love, but I ask you not to consider it a gift.

Please think of it as a loan. Then pay it back—with interest. You will only be the richer for doing so.

A portion of my advance from *Companions in Courage* was used to set up companions-in-courage.org, a Web resource intended for athletes, trainers, and everyday miracle workers to share their experiences and provide one another and all who visit with information and the power and support they need to achieve their individual dreams.

A portion was also donated to the Michael J. Fox Foundation for Parkinson's Research. The foundation raises national awareness of Parkinson's disease and the need for government support of Parkinson's research.

For more information, go to www.michaeljfox.org/#.

All of my earnings from sales of *Companions in Courage* are being donated to the National Hockey League's Hockey's All-Star Kids program.

Through the NHL's relationships with children's hospitals in Canada and the United States, Hockey's All-Star Kids program includes patient visits, fund-raising support, and programs to help create a positive environment for patients and their families.

For more information, see www.hockeysall-starkids.com.

Pat LaFontaine
October 2000

PAT LAFONTAINE

Center
Born 02-22-1965, St. Louis, MO
Height 5'10"
Weight 180 lbs.

Selected by New York Islanders first round, #3 overall 1983 NHL entry draft

Season	Team	Lge	Regular Season					Playoffs				
			GP	G	A	Pts	PIM	GP	G	A	Pts	PIM
1982–83	Verdun Juniors	QMJHL	70	104	130	234	10					
1983–84	NY Islanders	NHL	15	13	6	19	6	16	3	6	9	8
1984–85	NY Islanders	NHL	67	19	35	54	32	9	1	2	3	4
1985–86	NY Islanders	NHL	65	30	23	53	43	3	1	0	1	0
1986–87	NY Islanders	NHL	80	38	32	70	70	14	5	7	12	10
1987–88	NY Islanders	NHL	75	47	45	92	52	6	4	5	9	8
1988–89	NY Islanders	NHL	79	45	43	88	26	—	—	—	—	—
1989–90	NY Islanders	NHL	74	54	51	105	38	2	0	1	1	0
1990–91	NY Islanders	NHL	75	41	44	85	42	—	—	—	—	—
1991–92	Buffalo Sabres	NHL	57	46	47	93	98	7	8	3	11	4
1992–93	Buffalo Sabres	NHL	84	53	95	148	63	7	2	10	12	0
1993–94	Buffalo Sabres	NHL	16	5	13	18	2	—	—	—	—	—
1994–95	Buffalo Sabres	NHL	22	12	15	27	4	5	2	2	4	2
1995–96	Buffalo Sabres	NHL	76	40	51	91	36	—	—	—	—	—
1996–97	Buffalo Sabres	NHL	13	2	6	8	4	—	—	—	—	—
1997–98	NY Rangers	NHL	67	23	39	62	36	—	—	—	—	—
	NHL Totals		865	468	545	1013	552	69	26	36	62	36

About the Author

American-born PAT LAFONTAINE has enjoyed success at every level of hockey, competing brilliantly not only in the National Hockey League but on the international stage as well.

Named as both the regular-season and playoff MVP with Verdun of the Quebec Major Junior Hockey League, the quick-handed center was then selected third overall in the 1983 NHL entry draft by the New York Islanders. He spent the first part of the 1983–84 season playing for the United States national team and was the club's leading scorer at the 1984 Sarajevo Olympics.

In 1989–90, Pat became only the third Islanders player (Mike Bossy and Bryan Trottier were the others) to score fifty goals in a season. He finished with fifty-four.

Traded to Buffalo on October 25, 1991, Pat quickly established himself as a leader. He wore the captain's C for the club from 1992 to 1997, and for the 1994–95 season won the Bill Masterton Memorial Trophy, which honors perseverance and dedication to the sport. It was in Buffalo that he began the tireless work with children and charities that led to the creation of Companions in Courage.

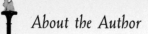 *About the Author*

Pat finished his NHL career with the New York Rangers (1997–98) and again played for the U.S. Olympic team, this time in Nagano, Japan, in 1998.

Pat always enjoyed international competition. He played on the American team that defeated Canada in the World Cup of Hockey in 1996 and also on the 1989 team at the World Championships. He also played on two Canada Cup teams (1987 and 1991).

On September 22, 2000, Pat was honored with the Patriots Award, given by the Congressional Medal of Honor Society.